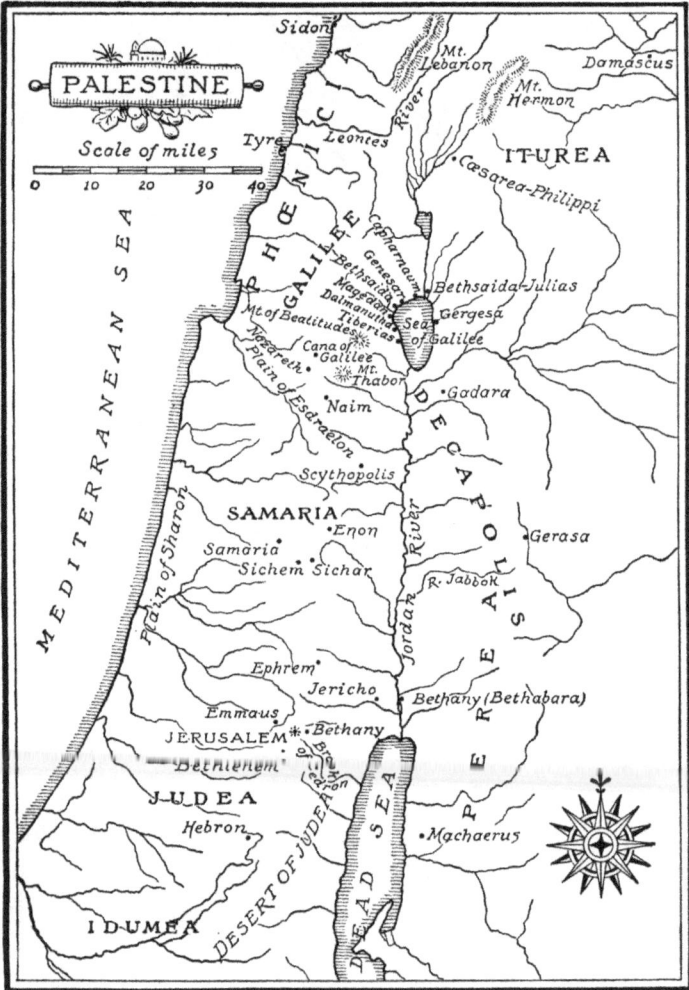

PALESTINE

Scale of miles

0   10   20   30   40

Sidon

Tyre

Leontes

PHOENICIA

GALILEE

Mt. Lebanon

Mt. Hermon

Damascus

Caesarea-Philippi

ITUREA

MEDITERRANEAN SEA

Capharnaum

Genesaret

Bethsaida

Magdala

Dalmanutha

Tiberias

Mt of Beatitudes

Cana of Galilee

Mt. Thabor

Nazareth

Plain of Esdraelon

Naim

Plain of Sharon

Scythopolis

SAMARIA

Enon

Samaria

Sichem Sichar

Ephrem

Jericho

Emmaus

JERUSALEM

Bethlehem

JUDEA

Hebron

IDUMEA

DESERT OF JUDEA

Brook Cedron

Bethany

Sea of Galilee

Bethsaida-Julias

Gergesa

Gadara

DECAPOLIS

Jordan River

R. Jabbok

Gerasa

PEREA

Bethany (Bethabara)

DEAD SEA

Machaerus

THE JOURNEYS OF JESUS

COMPILED FROM
THE GOSPEL NARRATIVE

BOOK ONE

BY

SISTER JAMES STANISLAUS
OF THE SISTERS OF ST. JOSEPH OF CARONDELET
ST. LOUIS, MISSOURI

WITH ILLUSTRATIONS AFTER BIDA

ST. AUGUSTINE ACADEMY PRESS
HOMER GLEN, ILLINOIS

Nihil Obstat

STI. LUDOVICI, DIE 4 OCTOBRIS 1927

JOANNES ROTHENSTEINER

CENSOR LIBRORUM

Imprimatur

STI. LUDOVICI, DIE 4 OCTOBRIS 1927

✠ JOANNES J. GLENNON

ARCHIEPISCOPUS

STI. LUDOVICI

This book was originally published in 1927
by Ginn and Company.

This facsimile edition was reproduced in 2025
by St. Augustine Academy Press.

ISBN: 978-1-64051-132-3

PREFACE

For Catholic children no story can be more important than that which tells of the Life, Death, and Resurrection of our Divine Lord. In many ways this story of Our Saviour has been told, and Catholic children in all countries and at all times have been moved by its recital. In the present series, the author follows the footsteps of the Messias from the time He leaves His home in Nazareth for the first time, on His public mission, and presents in a series of ten journeys the events of His Life.

Book One of "The Journeys of Jesus" deals with five of these ten journeys and covers a period extending from the Baptism of Jesus to the close of the second year of His public ministry.

Each event as narrated in the Gospel during this period forms a distinct topic in one chapter, given in the exact words as recorded in the New Testament. The descriptions of places and buildings given at the end of each chapter have been gathered from reliable sources. At the end of each narrative questions based on the text are included.

Maps and numerous illustrations form an attrac-

PREFACE

tive feature of the books and serve to impress and make clearer the lesson of the printed page. A Biblical Glossary of names with their pronunciation and definition is found at the end of each book.

The author wishes to express her deep appreciation and grateful acknowledgment to the B. Herder Book Company for permission to use the classification of places into journeys as given in the "Life of Jesus Christ," by A. J. Maas, of the Society of Jesus.

CONTENTS

PART I. THE BEGINNINGS OF THE PUBLIC MINISTRY OF JESUS

A FIRST JOURNEY OF JESUS

CONTENTS

CONTENTS

PART III. THE SECOND YEAR OF THE PUBLIC MINISTRY OF JESUS

A THIRD JOURNEY OF JESUS

CONTENTS

CONTENTS

THE JOURNEYS OF JESUS

BOOK ONE

PART I. THE BEGINNINGS
OF THE PUBLIC MINISTRY OF JESUS

A FIRST JOURNEY
OF JESUS

When Our Lord was about thirty years old, He left His home in Nazareth, and took the long road that led from Galilee to the river ford in Judea where John was baptizing.

Jesus had lived in Nazareth since He was brought back from Egypt by His Blessed Mother and St. Joseph. He had grown up in that place, had played there as a child, and as a young man had worked with St. Joseph in his carpenter's shop.

In those years He was preparing for the great work He had come on earth to do, but the Sacred Scriptures tell us nothing about the nature of the preparation. We know that He must have been an unusual boy, for St. Luke writes (ii, 40) that "the child grew, and waxed strong, . . . and the grace of God was in Him." One other story we know about His childhood—His journey to Jerusalem when He was twelve years old. There He was lost for three days and was found in the Temple by His Blessed Mother and St. Joseph, "sitting in the midst of the doctors, hearing them, and asking them questions." (St. Luke ii, 46.) These years are known as His hidden life. "And Jesus advanced in wisdom, and age, and grace with God and men." (St. Luke ii, 52.)

But this hidden life came to an end in the year 27 A.D. or early in the year following, when Our Lord left Nazareth for Judea. In the Sacred Scriptures we find no description of His departure from home. No picture is given us of His farewell to His Blessed Mother, but we may easily picture to ourselves what the parting must have been of such a Mother and such a Son, knowing that His hour had come.

If you will turn to the map of the Holy Land, on page ii, you may trace there the journey from Galilee to Judea. The road crossed a wide plain, called the Plain of Jezreel, passed under the walls of Scythopolis, and followed the mountains of Judea which border the Plain of Jordan on the west. The road then turned to the east, leaving Jericho on the right, and went down to the valley of the river. At the Jordan, near Bethany, was the place which John had chosen for the baptism of those who had heard his word.

After His Baptism Jesus, crossing the Jordan and the plain of Jericho, went to the desert of Judea. Following His fast of forty days and nights and His temptation, He returned to Bethany east of the Jordan, where John was still bearing witness to Him.

[6]

THE FIRST JOURNEY OF JESUS

Jesus remained there only a short time; then journeyed northward followed by Andrew and John, two disciples of the Baptist. The next morning Simon, the brother of Andrew, joined them. Jesus with these disciples turned toward Galilee, after Philip, and later Nathanael, had been added to the group.

They proceeded to Cana of Galilee, where a marriage feast took place. After the feast Jesus remained only a short time in Cana; then went on northward to Capharnaum, a distance of a day's journey, through roads that wind in and out among hills, always descending until the gorge opens on the lake and the green plain of Genesareth. The little group traveled through the villages of Magdala and Bethsaida and reached Capharnaum toward evening.

The chief things to be remembered about this first journey of Our Lord are:

> John's First Testimony to Jesus
> The Baptism of Jesus
> The Fast and Temptation of Jesus
> John's Second Testimony to Jesus
> John's Third Testimony to Jesus
> The Choosing of His First Disciples
> The Marriage Feast at Cana
> Jesus at Capharnaum

ST. JOHN IN THE DESERT

I

THE PRECURSOR OF JESUS

St. John the Baptist

The coming of Our Lord had long been foretold by the prophets, and it was expected that before the appearance of the Messias there would be forerunners to tell of His coming. It seems to have been commonly believed that Elias, who had been caught up to heaven, would return again to announce the advent of the Promised One. But it was St. John the Baptist who was chosen for this most important work.

We read in St. Luke's Gospel (i, 5–16): "There was in the days of Herod, the King of Judea, a certain priest named Zachary, . . . and his wife was of the daughters of Aaron, and her name Elizabeth. . . .

"And they had no son, . . . and they both were well advanced in years. . . .

"According to the custom of the priestly office, it was his lot to offer incense, going into the Temple of the Lord. . . .

"And there appeared to him an angel of the Lord, . . .

[9]

"And Zachary seeing him, was troubled, and fear fell upon him.

"But the angel said to him: Fear not, Zachary, for thy prayer is heard; and thy wife Elizabeth shall bear thee a son, and thou shalt call his name John:

"And thou shalt have joy and gladness, and many shall rejoice in his nativity.

"For he shall be great before the Lord; and shall drink no wine nor strong drink: and he shall be filled with the Holy Ghost, even from his mother's womb."

St. Luke writes in another verse (i, 80): "And the child grew, and was strengthened in spirit; and was in the deserts until the day of his manifestation to Israel."

St. Matthew writes in his Gospel (iii, 4): "And the same John had his garment of camels' hair, and a leathern girdle about his loins: and his meat was locusts and wild honey."

In preparation for his mission as the herald of Our Lord's coming, St. John had gone into the wilderness and, as we learn from St. Luke (iii, 1–2), began to announce the near approach of the Kingdom of God: "Now in the fifteenth year of the reign of Tiberius Cæsar, Pontius Pilate being governor of Judea, and Herod being tetrarch of Galilee, and Philip, his brother tetrarch of Iturea, and the country of Trachonitis, and Lysanias tetrarch of Abilina;

THE PRECURSOR OF JESUS

"Under the high priests Annas and Caiphas; the word of the Lord was made unto John, the son of Zachary, in the desert."

And when he "came into all the country about the Jordan, preaching the baptism of penance for the remission of sins," his strange dress and earnest speech aroused great interest and excitement among the people. They felt that this must be Elias who had returned from the heavens unto which he had been lifted up.

It was here that John began his great mission, "and his voice resounded in the land of Judea."

QUESTIONS

1. Who was John the Baptist?

2. Who were his parents?

3. What can you find in the Bible history about his birth and life?

4. How did he prepare himself to preach?

5. Where did he preach and baptize?

6. What did the people think of him?

7. When John began to preach and baptize who was governor of Judea?

8. Who was the Roman Emperor?

9. Where is Palestine? Bound it.

THE JOURNEYS OF JESUS

THE MISSION OF JOHN THE BAPTIST

John generally remained close to the river Jordan, and baptized his converts in one of the many streams that find their way into that famous river.

The prophets had urged the people to wash away the stains of sin while they purified their bodies. John required the whole body to be cleansed, and taught that the soul should be entirely flooded by sorrow for sin. He required that people should confess their sins before they were baptized, and persuaded them to repent of their evil ways, saying: "Do penance: for the Kingdom of Heaven is at hand." (St. Matthew iii, 2.)

When the throngs heard him as "A voice of one crying in the desert, Prepare ye the way of the Lord, make straight His paths," their hearts were stirred to more earnest longing for the coming of the promised Messias.

The people came from both sides of the Jordan, according to St. Matthew (iii, 5–6): "Then went out to him Jerusalem and all Judea, and all the country about Jordan:

"And were baptized by him in the Jordan, confessing their sins."

But not all who came gave evidence of true repentance. For St. Matthew (iii, 7) writes that when John saw many of the Pharisees and Sadducees coming to his baptism, he said to them: "Ye brood of vipers, who hath showed you to flee from the wrath to come?"

Never before had anyone dared to speak to these great ones of Jerusalem in such stern words. John, continuing, said to them: "Bring forth, therefore, fruit worthy of penance.

"And think not to say within yourselves, We have Abraham for our father. For I tell you that God is able of these stones to raise up children to Abraham.

"For now the axe is laid to the root of the trees. Every tree therefore that doth not yield good fruit, shall be cut down, and cast into the fire." (St. Matthew iii, 8–10.)

The Pharisees and Sadducees went from the Jordan angered, but not converted. Meanwhile the people's interest in the words and the work of John increased, and crowds gathered daily to hear his word and to prepare themselves for the coming of Jesus. So great was their admiration of John that according to St. Luke (iii, 15) many thought that "he might be the Christ."

John's First Testimony to Jesus

Even the common Jewish people expected the coming of a Redeemer, a Messias. Some of these people believed that John himself was the promised Redeemer.

But when John heard of this, he said: "I indeed baptize you with water; but there shall come One mightier than I, the latchet of Whose shoes I am not worthy to loose: He shall baptize you with the Holy Ghost, and with fire;

"Whose fan is in His hand, and He will purge His floor, and will gather the wheat into His barn; but the chaff He will burn with unquenchable fire.

"And many other things exhorting, did he preach to the people." (St. Luke iii, 15–18.)

When John said this he was talking about something which the people knew well. They had often seen the hard threshing floors on which the grain was trampled out by oxen or beaten out by flails. They knew also about the winnowing fan, which blew away the dirt and the husks and left the wheat. He did not need to tell them what he meant: that He Who was coming after him would divide the good—that is, the wheat—from the wicked—the chaff.

QUESTION

What virtue does John show in his answer to those who thought him to be the promised Redeemer?

II

THE BAPTISM OF JESUS

John had probably begun to preach in the month
of September. It was about three months afterward
that Our Lord followed the crowds from Galilee to
the Jordan.

The Baptist, although a near relative of Our Lord,
could not have seen Him since the days of childhood,
for he confesses, as we find in the Gospel of St. John
the Evangelist (i, 31), "And I knew Him not." It
may, then, have been by revelation from heaven, as
Our Saviour stood in the midst of the crowds, that
John recognized Jesus on the banks of the Jordan.

Who can imagine the feelings of John when he
saw the Sinless One enter with sinners into the water
and ask to be baptized like one of them! The God-
Man had become as one of the people. He obeyed
the word of John as if He were a sinner.

We cannot tell how Our Lord revealed Himself and
His mission to John, but that He did so we are not
left in doubt, for we read that the Baptist said in

deep humility: "I ought to be baptized by Thee, and comest Thou to me?

"And Jesus answering, said to him: Suffer it to be so now, for so it becometh us to fulfil all justice." (St. Matthew iii, 14–15.)

John hesitated no longer. With trembling reverence and childlike simplicity he baptized Jesus, his Lord and Master. "And forthwith coming up out of the water, He saw the heavens opened, and the Spirit as a Dove descending, and remaining on Him. And there came a Voice from heaven: Thou art My beloved Son; in Thee I am well pleased." (St. Mark i, 10–11.)

The baptism administered by John was not a sacrament, but was a figure of the Sacrament of Baptism whereby we are made Christians and children of God. The appearance of the Dove and the Voice from Heaven at the Baptism of Our Lord clearly showed that He was the Messias. The Baptism of Jesus is looked upon as part of the Feast of the Epiphany, or Manifestation, celebrated in the Church every year on January 6.

QUESTIONS

1. What did John require before baptism?

2. Where was Jesus baptized?

3. Was the baptism given by John a sacrament of the Church?

BAPTISM OF CHRIST

4. Give an example of how Jesus showed His humility.

5. What is the Holy Trinity?

6. What is the Dove the type of?

7. State the words of the Father at the Baptism of Jesus.

8. What are the effects of the Sacrament of Baptism on our souls?

9. Were all classes of people converted by John's preaching?

THE RIVER JORDAN

The Jordan is the only river in Palestine and is one of the most remarkable in the world. It rises at the base of Mount Hermon, passes southward through the country, and empties into the Dead Sea.

It is a deep and rapid river. About forty miles south of its source it enters the Lake of Genesareth. Its current here is so strong that it is said to pass through this lake without mixing with the lake water. Leaving this lake, the river flows south with many windings for a distance of ninety miles, where it falls into the Dead Sea. Its entire length is estimated to be about one hundred and fifty miles.

The Jordan is famous as the scene of several miraculous events. Its waters "stood in one place" to allow a passage for the Israelites on their journey from the desert (Josue iii, 16).

THE RIVER JORDAN

THE JOURNEYS OF JESUS

It was on the left bank of this river, at a place called Bethany or Bethabara, that John the Baptist preached to the multitudes, and Jesus came to be baptized.

BETHANIA BEYOND THE JORDAN

There were two places named Bethania. One was "Bethania beyond the Jordan," that is, on the east side of the river, where John baptized; the other Bethania, or Bethany, was a village about two miles east of Jerusalem. In this other Bethany lived Mary and Martha with their brother Lazarus, he whom Jesus raised to life. It was here, too, that Mary Magdalen poured the ointment on the Saviour's head.

EXERCISES

1. Find on the map the river Jordan and describe its course.

2. Point out on the map the two places called Bethany.

III

JESUS IS TEMPTED IN THE DESERT

THE THREE TEMPTATIONS

Immediately after the Baptism of Jesus He "was led by the Spirit into the desert, to be tempted by the devil. And when He had fasted forty days and forty nights, afterwards He was hungry.

"And the tempter coming said to Him: If Thou be the Son of God, command that these stones be made bread.

"Who answered and said: *It is written, Not in bread alone doth man live, but in every word that proceedeth from the mouth of God.*"

A second time the devil tempted Our Lord. "Then the devil took Him up into the Holy City, and set Him upon the pinnacle of the Temple,

"And said to Him: If Thou be the Son of God, cast Thyself down, for it is written: *That He hath given His angels charge over Thee, and in their hands shall they bear Thee up, lest perhaps Thou dash Thy foot against a stone.*"

To this temptation of Satan, Jesus answered: "It

"BEGONE, SATAN."

is written again: *Thou shalt not tempt the Lord thy God.*"

Then the devil made a third trial. He "took Him up into a very high mountain and showed Him all the kingdoms of the world and the glory of them,

"And said to Him: All these will I give Thee, if falling down Thou wilt adore me.

"Then Jesus saith to him: Begone, Satan: for it is written, *The Lord thy God shalt thou adore, and Him only shalt thou serve.*

"Then the devil left Him; and behold angels came and ministered to Him." (St. Matthew iv, 1–11.)

The Baptism and Temptation of Jesus seem to be two events which explain each other. The first was a manifestation of the Spirit of God; the other, of the Spirit of Evil. The first shows Jesus as the Son of the Most High; the other shows Him in His humanity subject to temptation by the devil, even as one of us to whom He became a brother by becoming Man.

QUESTIONS

1. How is Jerusalem spoken of in this lesson?

2. How does the Church commemorate the Forty Days' Fast of Jesus?

3. How many instances of a forty days' fast are given in the Old Testament?

4. Where did Jesus spend his forty days of fasting?

5. Show how we are more pleasing to God after we have overcome temptation than before.

6. How was the God-Man rewarded after His three temptations?

7. What is meant by the "pinnacle of the Temple"?

THE DESERT WHERE JESUS WAS TEMPTED

Père Didon, in his "Life of Christ," tells us that while the Gospel narratives do not precisely define the desert into which Jesus was led by the Spirit, they can only mean the desert of Judea. The most ancient tradition, he says, has always sought for and venerated the traces of Jesus in the wild and mountainous region which extends to the west above Jericho as far as the heights of Bethany.

Jesus, on leaving the Jordan, must have crossed the plain of Jericho, and leaving the town to the left, have climbed the steep slopes of the mountain now called the Quarantaine.

The place is at once a desert and a mountain, uniting in its grandeur both austerity and majesty. This was probably the place to which Jesus retired. The image of Christ as He was in life seems to haunt these hills.

JESUS IS TEMPTED IN THE DESERT

JERUSALEM

Jerusalem, the capital of Israel and afterwards of Judah, was situated in a district called the land of Moriah. It lay within the territory which had been given to the tribe of Benjamin when the Israelites first settled in Palestine. Later the tribe of Judah captured it. The city was built on three hills: Akra, Moriah, and Zion. The Jews called it the Holy City and the City of God, and it is still known in the East by this last name.

It is supposed to have been built at least as early as the time of Abraham and was one of those towns from which the Israelites could not drive out the Jebusites, who had built it. The Jebusites boasted that their lame and blind could defend its fort; but it was taken by David, who made it his residence (2 Kings, v, 6–9) and called it by his own name, the City of David.

In early times the city was divided into three parts: Salem (the lower or Old Town), afterwards called Akra; Zion, or the City of David; and the Temple. Bezetha (the New Town) was not built until after the time of Our Saviour. These divisions were separated from one another by walls and towers, and the whole city was surrounded by a high wall.

THE JOURNEYS OF JESUS

The hills on which the city stood were separated by deep valleys from the surrounding heights. East of the city was the vale of Jehosophat; south and southwest were the valleys of Gihon and Hinnom. The brook Cedron, or Kedron, flowed on the eastern side of the city, and the stream of Shiloah, or Gihon, on the southern side.

EXERCISES AND QUESTIONS

1. Locate Jerusalem on the map.

2. Find and locate the brook Cedron on the map on page ii.

3. Why is the plain of Jericho mentioned in this lesson?

4. By what different names is Jerusalem known?

IV

THE PRECURSOR'S TESTIMONIES

John's Testimony of Himself

The interest which John roused in the people round Bethany by his own life of penance, as well as by his announcement of the coming of the Messias, stirred up the members of the Sanhedrin. They did not like this fearless man, whose life was so unlike their own way of living, and whose rebuke to them was so severe. They were puzzled and disturbed by his appearance and preaching; so they sent to him certain Levites asking: "Who art Thou?

"And he confessed and did not deny: and he confessed: I am not the Christ.

"And they asked him: What then? Art thou Elias? And he said: I am not. Art thou the Prophet? And he answered: No.

"They said therefore unto him: Who art thou, that we may give an answer to them that sent us? What sayest thou of thyself?

"He said: *I am the voice of one crying in the wilderness, make straight the way of the Lord*, as said the prophet Isaias.

"And they that were sent, were of the Pharisees.

"And they asked him and said to him: Why then dost thou baptize, if thou be not Christ, nor Elias, nor the Prophet?

"John answered them, saying: I baptize with water; but there hath stood One in the midst of you Whom you know not.

"The same is He that shall come after me, Who is preferred before me: the latchet of Whose shoe I am not worthy to loose."

Such firmness and humility on the part of John in announcing One greater than himself disturbed the councilors of the Sanhedrin, who turned away, refusing to ask him any more questions. "These things were done in Bethania beyond the Jordan, where John was baptizing." (St. John i, 19–28.)

These Jews had the right to ask these questions of John. They had been sent by authorities whose duty it was to see that no new or false doctrines were taught. It was their manner of asking that was at fault. Their unbelief and malice betrayed their ill will toward John and his teachings.

However, their questions gave John an opportunity to proclaim to all that the Saviour was not only coming, but was actually there in the midst of them.

THE PRECURSOR'S TESTIMONIES

THE SANHEDRIN

The Sanhedrin was the chief court of the Jews. Its duties were to judge important cases, to decide what the Law meant, and to discuss religious and political affairs.

It was made up of seventy-two members, divided into three parts: (1) the Chamber of Priests, (2) the Chamber of Doctors and Scribes, and (3) the Chamber of Magistrates and Ancients. The first chamber was composed of the high priests and the heads of the twenty-four families from which the priests were chosen. Men who knew the Law made up the second chamber, while the members of the third chamber were magistrates and the chief men of the nation.

Joseph of Arimathea and Nicodemus were members of the Sanhedrin, though they took no part in the judgment of Jesus.

JOHN'S SECOND TESTIMONY TO JESUS

"The next day John saw Jesus coming to him and he saith: Behold the Lamb of God, behold Him Who taketh away the sins of the world.

"This is He, of Whom I said: After me there cometh a Man, Who is preferred before me: because He was before me.

[29]

"And I knew Him not, but that He may be made manifest in Israel, therefore am I come baptizing with water.

"And John gave testimony, saying: I saw the Spirit coming down, as a Dove from heaven, and He remained upon Him.

"And I knew Him not; but He Who sent me to baptize with water, said to me: He upon Whom thou shalt see the Spirit descending, and remaining upon Him, He it is that baptizeth with the Holy Ghost.

"And I saw, and I gave testimony, that this is the Son of God." (St. John i, 29–34.)

JOHN'S THIRD TESTIMONY TO JESUS

"The next day again John stood, and two of his disciples.

"And beholding Jesus walking, he saith: Behold the Lamb of God." (St. John i, 35–36.)

This was the first name given to Jesus on His entry into public life. No other expressed His inward and outward character of a victim to be sacrificed. He was "the Lamb led to the slaughter" because the Lord had "laid on Him the iniquity of us all," the innocent Victim who was to save all mankind by His atonement for their sins.

[30]

"BEHOLD THE LAMB OF GOD!"

THE JOURNEYS OF JESUS

QUESTIONS

1. What mistaken idea about John the Baptist did the people have?

2. Give some of the statements which John made about himself to correct these ideas.

3. In what words did John give testimony to Christ at three different times?

4. Are there men today who live as John the Baptist did?

5. What reason have they for leading such a life?

6. What was the Sanhedrin?

7. Name two men who were members of the Sanhedrin, yet friends of Jesus.

8. In what way did each show his respect for Christ?

V

JESUS CHOOSES HIS FIRST TWO DISCIPLES

ANDREW AND JOHN FOLLOW JESUS

Even while the Baptist was saying, "Behold the Lamb of God," the hearts of the two men with him were moved at the sight of Jesus. They felt that they should like to follow Him.

"And the two disciples heard him speak, and they followed Jesus.

"And Jesus turning, and seeing them following Him, saith to them: What seek you? Who said to Him, Rabbi, (which is to say, being interpreted, Master,) where dwellest Thou?

"He saith to them: Come and see. They came, and saw where He abode, and they stayed with Him that day: now it was about the tenth hour." (St. John i, 37–39.)

St. Andrew was one of these two disciples, as we learn from a verse later on in this same Gospel; it is believed that St. John the Evangelist, "the beloved disciple" and the writer of this account, was the other.

THE JOURNEYS OF JESUS

SIMON, PHILIP, AND NATHANAEL ARE CALLED

Pious readers of the Sacred Scriptures often wish that the inspired writers had set down in more detail the incidents in the life of Our Lord. For example, how briefly the four evangelists tell of the choosing of the Apostles, and how little is written of the feelings which urged these men to answer the Divine call—to leave all things and follow Christ. We are left to our own thoughts and imaginings as to all this.

We gather from St. John's Gospel (i, 41) that Andrew must have been eager, once he had found Jesus for himself, to make Him known to others: "He findeth first his brother Simon, and saith to him: We have found the Messias, which is, being interpreted, the Christ. And he brought him to Jesus."

Thus in a very few words is told the story of Andrew's desire to get a new recruit for the army of the Kingdom of Heaven. In words just as few and as simple we are told how this new disciple was chosen to be the leader of the Apostles: "And Jesus looking upon him, said: Thou art Simon the son of Jona: thou shalt be called Cephas, which is interpreted Peter." (St. John i, 42.)

Upon this Cephas, this Peter, this Rock (for these words all mean the same thing), our Divine Lord was later to build His Church, but the Evangelist barely gives the fact and passes on. Here at the very beginning we see Our Saviour doing something for Peter which He did for none other of the Apostles; that is, changing his name to a name that had deep meaning, as later events showed.

St. John continues (i, 43): "On the following day, He would go forth into Galilee, and He findeth Philip. And Jesus saith to him: Follow Me."

Philip too, like Andrew, was eager to let others know of his new-found Lord. The Gospel says: "Philip findeth Nathanael, and saith to him: We have found Him of whom Moses in the Law, and the prophets, did write, Jesus the son of Joseph of Nazareth.

"And Nathanael said to him: Can any thing of good come from Nazareth? Philip saith to him: Come and see.

"Jesus saw Nathanael coming to Him and He saith of him: Behold an Israelite indeed, in whom there is no guile.

"Nathanael saith to Him: Whence knowest Thou me? Jesus answered, and said to him: Before that Philip called thee, when thou wast under the fig tree, I saw thee.

"Nathanael answered Him, and said: Rabbi, Thou art the Son of God, Thou art the king of Israel.

"Jesus answered, and said to him: Because I said

unto thee, I saw thee under the fig tree, thou believest: greater things than these shalt thou see.

"And He saith to him: Amen, amen I say to you, you shall see the heaven opened, and the angels of God ascending and descending upon the Son of Man." (St. John i, 45–51.)

QUESTIONS

1. In what way did Andrew make known his faith in Christ?

2. Which Apostle received the first direct call from Christ?

3. Name the first five disciples of Jesus.

4. What particular virtue or quality do you think that each of these disciples had?

5. Who led Andrew and John to Christ?

6. Who can lead others to God by their teaching?

7. What words of praise did Jesus address to Nathanael?

THE VALLEY OF THE JORDAN

The plain or valley through which the Jordan flows was once rich and beautiful. In early days this valley was the pasture land chosen by Lot when he separated from Abraham. "And Lot, lifting up his eyes, saw all the country about the Jordan, which was watered throughout . . . as the paradise of the Lord." (Genesis xiii, 10.)

VI

THE MARRIAGE FEAST AT CANA

THE BEGINNING OF MIRACLES

And now Jesus and His five disciples traveled northward toward Nazareth. He was here in a place familiar to Him from boyhood, and it is to be supposed that His Blessed Mother and He, Himself, were well known to many in that region. So it does not surprise us when we learn from St. John that at Cana of Galilee the Mother of Jesus was present at a marriage feast. The house was possibly that of some friend or relative, and she had gone there before the arrival of Jesus. The Gospel tells us (St. John ii, 2): "And Jesus also was invited, and His disciples, to the marriage."

Such festivals lasted, among the Jews, for several days and were times of much rejoicing. But at this particular feast something happened which caused much trouble to the people of the house.

If you should go to a party and find that there were not enough refreshments for everybody, you would very likely feel that you were being entertained by people who had not taken much trouble in planning

[37]

the party. The Jews, at the time of Jesus, expected the family who were giving a wedding feast to have enough wine for everyone so long as the feast lasted. When a feast lasted several days, of course a great deal of wine was needed. Perhaps there were more guests at this wedding than the family had planned for. However it happened, the wine had given out before the feast was over.

The Gospel tells us: "The Mother of Jesus saith to Him: They have no wine. And Jesus saith to her: Woman, what is that to Me and to thee? my hour is not yet come."

By this, Jesus meant "the hour" set by His heavenly Father for Him to work His miracles in public. From the answer to His Blessed Mother it seemed as if He did not intend to do anything for her or for the master of the house; but, in spite of what seemed like a refusal, she was sure He would grant her request. She knew His infinite power. She knew that He would not refuse her. So she said to the waiters: "Whatsoever He shall say to you, do ye."

The Gospel goes on: "Now there were set there six waterpots of stone, according to the manner of the purifying of the Jews, containing two or three measures apiece.

"Jesus saith to them: Fill the waterpots with water. And they filled them up to the brim.

THE MARRIAGE FEAST AT CANA

"And Jesus saith to them: Draw out now, and carry to the chief steward of the feast. And they carried it.

"And when the chief steward had tasted the water made wine, and knew not whence it was, but the waiters knew who had drawn the water; the chief steward calleth the bridegroom,

"And saith to him: Every man at first setteth forth good wine, and when men have well drunk, then that which is worse. But thou hast kept the good wine until now." (St. John ii, 3–10.)

This changing of the water into wine at the marriage feast of Cana, St. John tells us, was the "beginning of miracles" done by Our Lord. By this miracle He "manifested His glory, and His disciples believed in Him." It was the first time that Our Saviour had revealed His power to them. And the miracle was done at His Mother's request.

By performing this miracle it may well be believed that Jesus wished us to know the influence with Him of His Mother's prayer; and since the miracle was performed at a wedding feast, we may know how holy marriage was and is in His sight. Furthermore, the changing of water into wine was a symbol of what takes place every day in Holy Mass, when, at the consecration, wine is changed into the Precious Blood of Jesus.

THE JOURNEYS OF JESUS

QUESTIONS

1. What did Our Saviour mean by saying: "My hour is not yet come?

2. From what she did at this feast, have we any reason to think that our Blessed Mother's words are powerful with her Divine Son?

3. What event have we in which a great miracle is daily performed?

CANA OF GALILEE

We do not know just where Cana of Galilee was. Tradition says that it was at Kefr Kenna, four miles southwest of Tiberias, on the road to Nazareth. Some, however, believe that 'Ain Kana, about eight miles north of Nazareth, on the ridge back of the plain of Asochis, is more probably the Cana called Cana of Galilee. Others think that Kanat-El Jelel is the place.

The town must have been of some importance in the days of Our Saviour. Cana was the home of Nathanael, but its greatest fame has come to it because it was the place where Our Lord performed His first miracle.

EXERCISES

1. Point out Galilee on the map.

2. Locate Nazareth.

3. Find Cana on the map.

VII

JESUS GOES TO CAPHARNAUM

The Mother and Brethren of Jesus

We do not know what reasons Jesus had for not returning to Nazareth after the marriage at Cana. All we are told in St. John's Gospel (ii, 12–13) is: "After this he went down to Capharnaum, He and His Mother, and His brethren, and His disciples: and they remained there not many days.

"And the Pasch of the Jews was at hand, and Jesus went up to Jerusalem."

The "brethren" mentioned here as accompanying Our Lord were not, of course, actually His brothers but His cousins, the children of Cleophas, the brother of St. Joseph. According to the usual style of the Scriptures they are called "brethren"; that is, near relatives of Our Saviour.

"They remained not many days" in Capharnaum; but, short as was Our Lord's stay in this place, He showed His power and preached and performed miracles. We know this from the words: "As great things as we have heard done in Capharnaum, do also here

THE MOTHER AND THE BRETHREN OF JESUS

in Thy own country." (St. Luke iv, 23.) What these deeds were that were known all over Galilee the Gospel does not tell us, but, judging from what is told us of His deeds in other places, we may well imagine that they were miracles of kindness and compassion. They surely included the healing of the sick, the cleansing of lepers, and the preaching of the good news of salvation to the poor and the sinful.

The time of "the Pasch of the Jews was at hand," and groups of pilgrims were gathering at all the cities and towns on the shores of the Lake of Genesareth. Jesus probably joined some caravan with pilgrims from Galilee, taking the road which started east of the Jordan and which led to Jerusalem by way of Bethany and the Mount of Olives.

QUESTIONS

1. Did Jesus show His power in any way during His short stay in Capharnaum?

2. What did the people of Nazareth say to Him of His works at Capharnaum?

3. Explain the meaning of "brethren."

CAPHARNAUM

Capharnaum was a city on the northern shore of the Lake of Genesareth. The city was surrounded by walls and had a tax office and a customhouse. Nothing remains of it today. It seems to have been an important town in Our Lord's time. He often stayed there, and so St. Matthew calls it "His own city." Peter, who was married, lived there, and possibly when Jesus dwelt there He stayed at the house of Peter's wife's mother.

From Capharnaum Jesus seems to have gone up and down through the neighboring towns on His mission. He preached in the synagogues, on the seashore, and on the hillsides. From the people of Capharnaum He chose many of His disciples, and in Capharnaum He worked some of His greatest miracles.

EXERCISE

Locate Capharnaum on the map.

THE PASCH

The Pasch, or Passover, was the first of the three great festivals of the Jews. It continued for eight days, beginning with the full moon which comes after the spring equinox.

It was held in remembrance of the night when all the first-born children of the Egyptians were killed and all the first-born children of the Jews were saved. At this feast the first fruits of the barley harvest were offered in the Temple.

PART II. THE FIRST YEAR
OF THE PUBLIC MINISTRY OF JESUS

A SECOND JOURNEY
OF JESUS

Jesus did not stay many days at Capharnaum. He celebrated in Jerusalem the Passover of the year 28, going then into the land of Judea as far as Idumea. When He heard that John the Baptist had been imprisoned, He left Judea and went again into Galilee, passing through Samaria. He spent two days in Samaria, in a place called Sichar. Then He visited again the place where He had been brought up, the town of Nazareth. Driven out of that town, He went to Cana and, after a short time, to Capharnaum. From this city He went forth into the towns of Galilee and returned again to Capharnaum.

The principal things to be remembered about this journey are:

> The First Purification of the Temple
> Christ's Talk with Nicodemus
> Christ's Ministry in Judea
> John's Imprisonment by Herod
> Jesus and the Samaritans
> The Preaching of Jesus in Galilee
> The Healing of the Ruler's Son

THE JOURNEYS OF JESUS

The Miraculous Draught of Fishes
The Healing of a Leper
The Cure of a Man with an Unclean Spirit
The Cure of Simon's Mother-in-law
The Healing of a Man Sick with the Palsy
The Calling of Levi

I

THE FIRST PURIFICATION OF THE TEMPLE

Jesus Drives the Buyers and Sellers from the Temple

When Jesus arrived in Jerusalem He went to the Temple and entered the outer court, which was called the Court of the Gentiles. There he found a crowd of people who had in many cases come long distances to take part in the Passover, or Pasch.

A number of these Jews, who had come from Roman provinces, had money stamped with images of idols. The things necessary for the Jewish sacrifices could not be bought with such money, so it had to be exchanged for the coin used in the Temple. Money-changers had set up tables in the Court, where this foreign money was exchanged for the sacred coin. This exchanging was lawful and necessary, but many of the money-changers had been cheating the pilgrims.

Dealers brought droves of oxen and flocks of sheep and lambs; sellers of doves had their places near the stands of those who sold oil, incense, salt, and all things needed for the altar service. There was much noisy coming and going, with disputes over money-changing and sales, and these, added to the cries and bellowing of the animals, made of the sacred Court a market place rather than a place of worship and prayer. The trading itself was not wrong, since the things bought and sold and the money exchanged were all necessary in providing for the sacrifices, but it should have been done outside the gate of the Temple.

The guardians of the Temple not only allowed this trading, but even encouraged it. Many pious souls must have been grieved to see the holy place used in this way. We may be sure that many times our Divine Lord saw this trading and was sad. So He took this occasion to teach a lesson to those who were engaged in it. St. John writes (ii, 15–17): "And when He had made, as it were, a scourge of little cords, He drove them all out of the Temple, the sheep also and the oxen; and the money of the changers He poured out, and the tables He overthrew.

"And to them that sold doves He said: Take these things hence, and make not the House of My Father a house of traffic.

"And His disciples remembered, that it was written: *The zeal of Thy House hath eaten Me up.*"

JESUS DRIVING THE BUYERS AND SELLERS OUT OF THE TEMPLE

Full of anger, the people whose business suffered from this act of Jesus demanded by what right He did these things. They said to Him: "What sign dost Thou show unto us, seeing Thou dost these things?

"Jesus answered, and said to them: Destroy this Temple, and in three days I will raise it up.

"The Jews then said: Six and forty years was this Temple in building; and wilt Thou raise it up in three days?

"But He spoke of the temple of His Body." (St. John ii, 18–21.)

QUESTIONS

1. By what words at the purification of the Temple did Jesus show His Divinity and authority?

2. Who said these words: "What sign dost Thou show unto us, seeing Thou dost these things?"

3. What did they mean by "these things"?

4. Why did the Pharisees take offense at the purification of the Temple?

5. Why was it necessary to have money-changers in the Temple?

6. How long did the Feast of the Pasch last?

7. Explain what Jesus meant by these words: "Destroy this Temple, and in three days I will raise it up."

THE PURIFICATION OF THE TEMPLE

THE TEMPLE

The Temple was a group of buildings in the form of a square. They were built one inside the other on rising ground, so that the central building, or holy place, was the highest of all. The outside wall was high, but the inner walls and their beautiful gates could be seen above it. The Temple grounds, which covered nearly twenty acres, had been built up by immense walls of stone from the valley below, so that they were level.

The outer court, called the Court of the Gentiles, took up about two thirds of the space in the Temple. Along its inner sides ran rows of pillars which formed porches. In these porches devout people prayed and worshiped. In the same porches traders or hucksters had been allowed to sell the goods needed in the Temple for the Jewish sacrifices, and foreign coin was exchanged there, as we have seen, for the Jewish money, which alone was accepted in the Temple.

II

NICODEMUS VISITS JESUS

Jesus Explains the Necessity of Baptism and Foretells the Manner of His Death

"And there was a man of the Pharisees, named Nicodemus, a ruler of the Jews." (St. John iii, 1.)

Nicodemus was a Pharisee and a member of the Sanhedrin. He was honest and religious, and he wanted to know the truth. He had listened to Our Lord's teaching in and around Jerusalem and had seen His miracles. He had made up his mind that Jesus was a great prophet, perhaps even the promised Messias. He wished to learn for himself who Our Lord really was, so he asked to see and speak to Him alone. We learn from the Gospels that he came to Jesus "by night." Why by night? Perhaps because he wished to speak quietly with Our Saviour, away from the crowds which gathered to hear Him by day. It may have been because he feared to let people know that he had anything to do with Our Lord.

When Nicodemus came to Jesus, he said: "Rabbi, we know that Thou art come a teacher from God;

for no man can do these signs which Thou dost, unless God be with him.

"Jesus answered, and said to him: Amen, amen I *say to thee*, unless a man be born again, he cannot see the Kingdom of God.

"Nicodemus saith to him: How can a man be born when he is old? can he enter a second time into his mother's womb, and be born again?

"Jesus answered: Amen, amen I say to thee, unless a man be born again of water and the Holy Ghost, he cannot enter into the Kingdom of God.

"That which is born of the flesh, is flesh; and that which is born of the Spirit, is spirit.

"Wonder not that I said to thee, you must be born again.

"The Spirit breatheth where He will; and thou hearest His voice, but thou knowest not whence He cometh, and whither He goeth: so is every one that is born of the Spirit.

"Nicodemus answered, and said to Him: How can these things be done?

"Jesus answered, and said to him: Art thou a master in Israel, and knowest not these things?

"Amen, amen I say to thee, that we speak what we know, and we testify what we have seen, and you receive not our testimony.

"If I have spoken to you earthly things, and you

believe not; how will you believe, if I shall speak to you heavenly things?

"And no man hath ascended into heaven, but He that descended from heaven, the Son of Man Who is in heaven.

"And as Moses lifted up the serpent in the desert, so must the Son of Man be lifted up.

"That whosoever believeth in Him, may not perish; but may have life everlasting.

"For God so loved the world, as to give His only begotten Son; that whosoever believeth in Him, may not perish, but may have life everlasting.

"For God sent not His Son into the world, to judge the world, but that the world may be saved by Him.

"He that believeth in Him is not judged. But he that doth not believe, is already judged: because he believeth not in the name of the only begotten Son of God.

"And this is the judgment: because the Light is come into the world, and men loved darkness rather than the light: for their works were evil.

"For every one that doth evil hateth the light, and cometh not to the light, that his works may not be reproved.

"But he that doth truth, cometh to the light, that his works may be made manifest, because they are done in God." (St. John iii, 2–21.)

NICODEMUS VISITS JESUS

St. John does not tell us what Nicodemus replied to these words. We do know that later on, when the enemies of Our Lord were seeking to destroy Him, Nicodemus reminded them that according to Jewish law no man could be condemned without first having a hearing. We also know that he was one of those who, after the crucifixion, took the body of Jesus from the cross and reverently laid it in the tomb.

QUESTIONS

1. What man was attracted by the teachings and miracles of Jesus and came to see Him by night?

2. "Born of water and the Holy Ghost" refers to what Sacrament?

3. What important truth necessary for eternal life did Jesus make known to Nicodemus?

4. In what city did the meeting between Jesus and Nicodemus take place?

5. Have we any reason to think that Nicodemus was grateful to Jesus for instructing him?

6. Write a short paragraph about the brazen serpent.

7. Why did Our Saviour speak to Nicodemus of the brazen serpent?

8. In what way should we imitate Nicodemus?

9. What do you admire in Nicodemus?

III

CHRIST'S MINISTRY IN JUDEA

The Disciples of Jesus Baptize

When the Feast of the Passover was ended, "Jesus and His disciples came into the land of Judea: and there He abode with them, and baptized." (St. John iii, 22.)

He stayed in Judea several months, visiting many towns and traveling as far south as Idumea.

Jesus was born in Judea; in the desert of Judea His coming had been announced by John the Baptist; the Temple was in Judea; and it was in Judea that Jesus began His teaching.

Crowds followed Him. The news of His miracles first interested them; then the wonderful words that fell from His lips; and finally His own goodness. But some of those who came did not—at least at first—understand His mission. Some of the disciples of John the Baptist, not understanding that John was only the forerunner of Jesus, complained to him that great multitudes were following Our Lord and were listening to Him. They said to John: "Rabbi, He that was with thee beyond the Jordan, to Whom thou gavest testimony, behold He baptizeth, and all men come to Him."

What sorrow must have filled the great heart of the Baptist as he listened to these envious words of his disciples! He answered: "A man cannot receive any thing, unless it be given him from heaven.

"You yourselves do bear me witness, that I said, I am not Christ, but that I am sent before Him.

"He that hath the bride, is the bridegroom: but the friend of the bridegroom, who standeth and heareth him, rejoiceth with joy because of the bridegroom's voice. This my joy therefore is fulfilled. . . .

"He that cometh from above, is above all. . . . "For He Whom God hath sent, speaketh the words of God: . . .

"The Father loveth the Son: and He hath given all things into His hand.

"He that believeth in the Son, hath life everlasting; but he that believeth not the Son, shall not see life; but the wrath of God abideth on him." (St. John iii, 26–36.)

John's Fourth Testimony to Jesus

John the Baptist took this opportunity to give his fourth testimony that Christ is the "Son of God."

Perhaps he knew that this was his farewell address

THE JOURNEYS OF JESUS

to his disciples. In noble and beautiful words he praised Jesus, saying: "He must increase [in the esteem of men], but I must decrease." (St. John iii, 30.)

QUESTIONS

1. Did Our Saviour baptize?

2. Were the disciples of John as unselfish as he was?

3. Where can we find the words of John, giving his fourth testimony to Jesus?

THE LAND OF JUDEA

Judea was one of the five parts of Palestine. It was the largest and most important part, stretching south to Idumea. Samaria bounded it on the north, on the east was the river Jordan, and the Mediterranean Sea lay on the west. The land along the coast was rich and more level than that inland, which was mountainous.

The Jews of Judea thought that they were better educated than the people of any other province of Palestine.

Many of the most famous places mentioned in the Holy Scriptures are in Judea—Bethlehem, Hebron, Jericho, and greatest of all, Jerusalem.

CHRIST'S MINISTRY IN JUDEA

John is Imprisoned by Herod

At that time Herod Antipas was the ruler of Galilee and Perea, under the Roman Emperor. He was not a real king, but he had power to deal with the conduct of the Jewish people.

His life was unworthy of his high position. He was living wickedly, for he had put away his own wife and had married Herodias, the wife of his brother. John the Baptist loved justice and hated sin, and he made Herod angry by declaring that it was not lawful for the king and Herodias to be living as man and wife. Herod was afraid of John, because the people looked upon the Baptist as a great prophet. Herod feared that John might influence the people against their king. He began to think of putting John to death, and so getting rid of him. He was urged on by Herodias, who hated the Baptist for what he had said about her wickedness. Therefore Herod had his soldiers seize John and imprison him in the fortress of Machærus, east of the Dead Sea.

Although Herod was angry with the Baptist he did not put him to death at once. He allowed John's disciples to see and talk with their leader. St. Mark tells us that even Herod himself, knowing John to be a just and holy man, "heard him willingly."

THE JOURNEYS OF JESUS

When John the Baptist fell into the hands of Herod, his public ministry came to an end. His work as a forerunner was done. He had been the voice crying in the wilderness. He had been the witness to Our Lord as the Son of God. And now that the work of Jesus had begun, there was no longer need of a herald.

While John was still in prison Our Lord said of him: "But what went you out to see? a prophet? Yea, I say to you, and more than a prophet," and "Amongst those that are born of women, there is not a greater prophet than John the Baptist." (St. Luke, vii, 26–28.)

QUESTIONS

1. Why was John the Baptist put in prison?

2. What did Herod think of John?

3. Do you think that the Pharisees, whom John had made angry, had anything to do with his arrest?

4. How did Our Lord speak of John the Baptist?

5. Where do we read of "a voice crying in the wilderness"?

THE FORTRESS OF MACHÆRUS

The prison of Machærus, built by Alexander, the son of Hyrcanus I, was destroyed by Gabinus and rebuilt by Herod. It served as a natural defense against the Arabs. The place was steep and high, nearly three quarters of a mile above the Dead Sea, and almost impossible to reach.

"The foundations of the citadel are still there, with a cistern and an underground chamber or cell which might have been the prison cell of John the Baptist. From this fortress one beholds the black waters of the Dead Sea and the mountains of Judea. The ruins round about show traces of Greek civilization." (Josephus, Jewish War, vii, 6.)

QUESTIONS

1. Find Machærus on the map.

2. What Jewish historian gives an account of this fortress?

3. Name the principal facts mentioned in the life of John the Baptist.

4. Was John the Baptist a martyr?

5. If so, in what sense was he one?

CHRIST AND THE WOMAN OF SAMARIA

IV

JESUS AND THE SAMARITANS

Christ and the Woman of Samaria

"And when Jesus had heard that John was delivered up, He retired into Galilee." (St. Matthew iv,
12.) In these words the Gospel tells us why Our Lord
with His disciples left Judea, where He had been
teaching and performing miracles.

When the Master went into Galilee He did not
take the road along the Jordan, but the shorter and
more direct road through Samaria. On this route
Our Saviour "cometh therefore to a city of Samaria,
which is called Sichar." This place was about forty
miles north of Jerusalem and near the land which
Jacob gave to his son Joseph.

Jacob's well was there, and Jesus, being tired, sat
by the well. It was about the sixth hour, that is,
about noon. His disciples had left Him and had gone
into Sichar to buy food. While Jesus was thus alone
a woman of Samaria came to draw water from the well.

When she had drawn up some water, Jesus said to
her: "Give Me to drink."

[65]

She knew from His language that He was a Judean, so she said to Him: "How dost Thou, being a Jew, ask of me to drink, who am a Samaritan woman? For the Jews do not communicate with the Samaritans.

"Jesus answered, and said to her: If thou didst know the Gift of God, and Who He is that saith to thee, Give Me to drink; thou perhaps wouldst have asked of Him, and He would have given thee living water.

"The woman saith to Him: Sir, Thou hast nothing wherewith to draw, and the well is deep; from whence then hast Thou living water?

"Art Thou greater than our father Jacob, who gave us the well, and drank thereof himself, and his children, and his cattle?

"Jesus answered, and said to her: Whosoever drinketh of this water, shall thirst again; but he that shall drink of the Water that I will give him, shall not thirst for ever:

"But the water that I will give him, shall become in him a fountain of water springing up into life everlasting.

"The woman saith to Him: Sir, give me this water, that I may not thirst, nor come hither to draw."

Jesus saw that she did not understand what He meant by "living water"; she did not know that he was talking of Divine grace. In order that she might see the truth He said to her: "Go, call thy husband, and come hither."

Now this woman had led a sinful life, and at the mention of her husband she may have felt afraid.

"The woman answered, and said: I have no husband. Jesus said to her: Thou hast said well, I have no husband:

"For thou hast had five husbands: and he whom thou now hast is not thy husband. This thou hast said truly."

Astonished that this stranger should know her past and present life so well, she said to Our Lord: "Sir, I perceive that Thou art a prophet." Then she spoke of the difference between the Jews and the Samaritans, saying: "Our fathers adored on this mountain, and you say that at Jerusalem is the place where men must adore."

"Jesus saith to her: Woman, believe Me, that the hour cometh, when you shall neither on this mountain nor in Jerusalem adore the Father.

"You adore that which you know not: we adore that which we know; for salvation is of the Jews.

"But the hour cometh, and now is, when the true adorers shall adore the Father in spirit and in truth. For the Father also seeketh such to adore Him.

"God is a Spirit; and they that adore Him, must adore Him in spirit and in truth.

[67]

"The woman saith to Him: I know that the Messias cometh (Who is called Christ); therefore, when He is come, He will tell us all things.

"Jesus saith to her: I am He, Who am speaking with thee."

Thus our merciful Saviour revealed Himself to this sinful woman, and she, forgetting all about the waterpot she had filled, hurried off into the city, calling to everyone she met: "Come, and see a Man Who has told me all things whatsoever I have done. Is not He the Christ?" And the people of the place, stirred by this news, came out of the city to see Our Lord.

Meanwhile His disciples had returned from the town, and wondered when they saw Him talking to the woman. They had brought back food. Now they offered it to Our Lord, saying, "Rabbi, eat.

"But He said to them: I have meat to eat, which you know not.

"The disciples therefore said one to another: Hath any man brought Him to eat?

"Jesus saith to them: My meat is to do the will of Him that sent Me, that I may perfect His work." (St. John iv, 3–34.)

Let us note how this woman draws by degrees nearer to the truth, nearer to a real faith in the Saviour. She first calls Him a Jew. Then she addresses Him respectfully as "Sir." Then He becomes to her a "prophet," and finally she runs to her neighbors and exclaims of Him: "Is not He the Christ?"

QUESTIONS

1. Finish this quotation: "If thou didst know the Gift of God . . . ."

2. Where did the conversation with the Samaritan woman take place?

3. What events in the Old Testament can you connect with this place?

4. "My meat is to do the will of Him that sent Me." Where and to whom were these words used?

5. Why did the Samaritan woman believe Jesus to be a prophet?

6. What particular virtue did the Samaritan woman show after she had talked with Jesus, in going to the city to tell of the Saviour?

7. In what way can we imitate her example?

SAMARIA AND THE SAMARITANS

Samaria was the smallest part of Palestine, lying between Judea and Galilee. It contained some of the richest lands of Palestine. The historian Josephus speaks of "its fruits and pastures, the milk of its flocks, and the abundance of its water-springs."

There was a road through Samaria from Judea to

Galilee. This, though often dangerous to travel on, was shorter and more direct than the road along the Jordan.

When the ten tribes were carried away by the Assyrians, the land of Israel was left nearly empty. Heathen people came to live there, and some of the Israelites returned from neighboring countries. In time these people became the Samaritans. They kept much of the religion of Moses, but they added to it parts of the heathen worship. The Jews thought that the Samaritans did not have the true faith, and so they disliked them. The Samaritans thought that the Jewish faith was not the true one.

The Jews would not allow the Samaritans to worship at Jerusalem. The Samaritans, therefore, built themselves a temple on Mount Gerizim, near Shechem, and worshiped there. The one thing which both Jews and Samaritans believed was that a Messias would come some day. The Jews thought that he would be a national hero. The Samaritans' idea of the Messias was a religious one.

THE SAMARITANS COME TO JESUS

We have seen that, after hearing the words of the Samaritan woman, the people of Sichar came out of the city, seeking Our Lord.

JESUS AND THE SAMARITANS

It was then that Our Saviour said to His disciples: "Do not you say, There are yet four months, and then the harvest cometh? Behold, I say to you, lift up your eyes, and see the countries; for they are white already to harvest." Our Lord was speaking, of course, of the harvest of souls—the spiritual harvest which was to be reaped by the Apostles and those that followed them, after He had ascended into heaven.

Again He said: "For in this is the saying true: That it is one man that soweth, and it is another that reapeth.

"I have sent you to reap that in which you did not labor; others have labored, and you have entered into their labors." By "others" Jesus plainly meant the patriarchs and prophets, whose words had been sown, like seed, in the hearts of the people of that region in years gone by. These words were now about to bear fruit at the voice of Jesus and under the teaching of His disciples.

There is no doubt that the Samaritans, as well as the disciples, listened eagerly to these words. We are told that "many more believed in Him because of His own word"; so much so, that they said to the woman: "We now believe, not for thy saying: for we ourselves have heard Him and know that This is indeed the Saviour of the world." (St. John iv, 35–42.)

THE JOURNEYS OF JESUS

Jesus must have been much pleased with the simple faith of these people. Unlike the Jews, who would not believe unless they saw signs and miracles, these Samaritans, at the first sight of the Saviour and at the sound of His voice, believed His Word.

QUESTIONS

1. In what way was the faith of the Samaritans different from that of the Jews?

2. Explain Christ's words "white already to harvest."

3. What men had preached before the coming of Christ?

4. Who were to continue teaching and preaching after Christ had ascended into heaven?

5. At the present time who continue to teach and preach His truths?

6. When we listen to sermons or to the priests explaining our Holy Religion, which group are we like: the Samaritans or the Jews of Christ's time?

7. Locate Samaria on the map.

8. Point out Sichar on the map.

V

JESUS PREACHES IN GALILEE

The People are Angered at His Words

St. John writes (iv, 43): "Now after two days, He departed thence, and went into Galilee." And the Galileans received Him with honor, having seen all that He had done in Jerusalem on the festival day, for they also had been in Jerusalem on that day.

St. Luke tells us (iv, 15) that on this journey into Galilee our Divine Lord "taught in their synagogues, and was magnified by all." In His own city of Nazareth He went into the synagogue, according to His custom on the Sabbath day; and He rose up to read.

"And the book of Isaias the prophet was delivered unto Him. And as He unfolded the book, He found the place where it was written:

"The Spirit of the Lord is upon me. Wherefore He hath anointed me to preach the Gospel to the poor, He hath sent me to heal the contrite of heart,

"To preach deliverance to the captives, and sight to the blind, to set at liberty them that are bruised, to preach the acceptable year of the Lord, and the day of reward.

JESUS IN THE SYNAGOGUE

"And when He had folded the book, He restored it to the minister, and sat down. And the eyes of all in the synagogue were fixed on Him.

"And He began to say to them: This day is fulfilled this Scripture in your ears.

"And all gave testimony to Him: and they wondered at the words of grace that proceeded from His mouth, and they said: Is not this the Son of Joseph?

"And He said to them: Doubtless you will say to Me this similitude: Physician, heal Thyself: as great things as we have heard done in Capharnaum, do also here in Thy own country.

"And He said: Amen I say to you, that no prophet is accepted in his own country.

"In truth I say to you, there were many widows in the days of Elias in Israel, when heaven was shut up three years and six months, when there was a great famine throughout all the earth.

"And to none of them was Elias sent, but to Sarepta of Sidon, to a widow woman.

"And there were many lepers in Israel in the time of Eliseus the prophet: and none of them was cleansed but Naaman the Syrian.

"And all they in the synagogue, hearing these things, were filled with anger.

"And they rose up and thrust Him out of the city; and they brought Him to the brow of the hill, whereon their city was built, that they might cast Him down headlong.

"But He, passing through the midst of them, went His way." (St. Luke iv, 16–30.)

QUESTIONS

1. Were the people of Nazareth glad to see Jesus?

2. Where did He go on the Sabbath day?

3. What was the lesson for that day? Quote the words of the Prophet Isaias.

4. What were the words of Jesus which displeased the Jews on this Sabbath?

5. How did they try to harm Jesus?

6. Did they succeed in doing this?

7. They wanted a miracle. Did Jesus give them one?

GALILEE AND THE GALILEANS

The kings of Syria divided the land of Israel west of the Jordan into three parts: Galilee, Samaria, and Judea. These divisions were adopted by the Romans and were used in Our Lord's time. Galilee is a fertile part of Palestine. It has much natural beauty and must have been a very flourishing country in the days when Our Lord was on earth.

The men of Galilee were brave and warlike. But in spite of their patriotism the Jews of Judea looked

JESUS THRUST OUT OF NAZARETH

down on them and made fun of their speech. It was to the Galileans, however, and not to the Judeans that Christ directed His first missionary labors and it was from its farmers, its fishermen, and its tax gatherers that He chose His first disciples.

NAZARETH

Nazareth, which will always be remembered by Christians as the place where Jesus spent his boyhood, is a town which stands in a hilly part of Galilee. The town itself is built in a hollow in the midst of the hills. The situation is beautiful, and the town is attractive. It has many fig and olive trees, and is noted for its lovely flowers. Its people are now mostly Christians, who have a fine church building, known as the Church of the Annunciation. There is a beautiful spring called St. Mary's Well; and many places connected with the life of Our Lord, His Blessed Mother, and St. Joseph are pointed out to visitors.

QUESTIONS

1. On the map find Judea, Samaria, and Galilee.
2. In which of these parts is Nazareth?

VI

JESUS IN CANA OF GALILEE

Jesus Heals the Ruler's Son

Jesus, driven from Nazareth, lived for a while at
Cana. "He came again therefore into Cana of Galilee, where He made the water wine." (St. John iv,
46.) His Blessed Mother may have been still living
with relatives and friends in Cana.

Cana is about twenty-four miles from Capharnaum,
and it is very likely that the name and the miracles
of Jesus had spread as far as the cities round the
lake on the shores of which Capharnaum is built. At
any rate, news must have reached that city that Jesus
was not far away; for we read that a certain ruler
came from Capharnaum to ask Jesus to cure his son,
who was sick. "He having heard that Jesus was
come from Judea into Galilee, went to Him and
prayed Him to come down and heal his son: for he
was at the point of death.

"Jesus therefore said to him: Unless you see signs
and wonders, you believe not."

This seemed to be refusing the father's prayer;

but something in the look or tone of Jesus must have encouraged the ruler, for again he said to Our Lord: "Lord, come down before that my son die." Jesus therefore said to him: "Go thy way; thy son liveth." This ruler was a man of faith. He did not question the goodness and power of Our Lord. He went home, as Jesus had told him to do.

"And as he was going down, his servants met him; and they brought word, saying, that his son lived.

"He asked therefore of them the hour wherein he grew better. And they said to him: Yesterday, at the seventh hour, the fever left him.

"The father therefore knew, that it was at the same hour that Jesus said to him: Thy son liveth; and himself believed, and his whole house." (St. John iv, 46–54.)

QUESTIONS

1. Where was Jesus when the ruler came to Him?

2. Where was the ruler's son?

3. "Go thy way; thy son liveth." Where and to whom were these words said?

4. What lesson did Jesus wish to teach the ruler of Capharnaum by not going to his son?

5. In what direction from Cana is Capharnaum?

VII

JESUS NEAR THE LAKE OF GENESARETH

THE LAKE OF GENESARETH

The Lake of Genesareth, called in the Old Testament the Sea of Chinnereth, is a body of water about fourteen miles long and six miles broad. The River Jordan widens out to form this lake and then, becoming a river again, flows on to the Dead Sea. The waters of the lake are clear and contain many fish. The shores are pleasing to the eye. On the east the lake is bounded by mountains. It is six hundred and fifty-three feet below the level of the Mediterranean Sea. Because it is so low its climate is almost tropical: the heat is intense in summer and great even in early spring. St. Luke alone calls it the Lake of Genesareth. The other evangelists call it the Sea of Tiberias or the Sea of Galilee.

BETHSAIDA

Bethsaida of Galilee was a fishing-village on the lake shore, to the northwest, near a little bay which gave good shelter for boats. Of this ancient Bethsaida only ruins remain to mark the town where lived five of the disciples: Andrew, Philip, Peter, James, and John.

THE MIRACULOUS DRAUGHT OF FISHES

"And it came to pass, that when the multitudes pressed upon Him to hear the Word of God, He stood by the Lake of Genesareth,

"And saw two ships standing by the lake: but the fishermen were gone out of them, and were washing their nets.

"And going into one of the ships that was Simon's, He desired him to draw back a little from the land. And sitting He taught the multitudes out of the ship.

"Now when He had ceased to speak, He said to Simon: Launch out into the deep, and let down your nets for a draught.

"And Simon answering said to Him: Master, we have labored all the night, and have taken nothing: but at Thy word I will let down the net.

"And when they had done this, they enclosed a very great multitude of fishes, and their net broke.

"And they beckoned to their partners that were in the other ship, that they should come and help them. And they came and filled both the ships so that they were almost sinking.

"Which when Simon Peter saw, he fell down at Jesus' knees saying: Depart from me, for I am a sinful man, O Lord.

"For he was wholly astonished, and all that were with him, at the draught of the fishes which they had taken.

"And so were also James and John the sons of Zebedee, who were Simon's partners. And Jesus saith to Simon: Fear not: from henceforth thou shalt catch men.

"And having brought their ships to land, leaving all things, they followed Him." (St. Luke v, 1–11.)

After the first call these disciples had given Jesus but a part of their time. Now at this second call they felt entirely bound to the service of the Divine Master Who had chosen them from among all men.

In the miraculous draught of fishes may be found many symbols of Christ and His Church. For example, the ship itself stands for the Church, with Our Lord as its Captain; the fishermen stand for the disciples; and the fish of all kinds, good and bad, stand for those who are caught in the net of the Church's teaching.

THE JOURNEYS OF JESUS

QUESTIONS

1. Who said, and on what occasion, "Master, we have labored all the night, and have taken nothing"?

2. What happened when they obeyed Jesus' words "Let down your nets"?

3. Finish this speech: "Depart from me . . . "

4. What miracle happened on the Sea of Galilee?

5. Name the four Apostles who were chosen near this sea.

6. When did Jesus say "From henceforth thou shalt catch men"?

7. What symbols can you find in the miraculous draught of fishes?

JESUS HEALS A LEPER

Jesus had been busy preaching and healing until long after sundown on the Sabbath day. The next day, we are told by St. Mark (i, 35–37), He rose very early, and "going out, He went into a desert place: and there He prayed.

"And Simon, and they that were with him, followed after Him.

"And when they had found Him, they said to Him: All seek for Thee."

Jesus knew that they sought Him because of the cures He had worked, and He wished to teach them that He was not sent for the curing of bodily diseases only, but also to heal diseases of the soul. So He said to them: "Let us go into the neighboring towns and cities, that I may preach there also; for to this purpose am I come.

"And He was preaching in their synagogues, and in all Galilee, and casting out devils." (St. Mark i, 38–39.)

This mission was short, perhaps less than a month. The Gospel tells us that after some days Jesus returned to Capharnaum. Only a single event of the mission in Galilee is told. It is the cure of a leper.

Leprosy was so horrible a disease that under the Old Law the leper was sent away from home and forbidden to enter the city. If a leper saw anyone coming toward him, he had to cry aloud the warning "Unclean! unclean!"

St. Luke writes of this leper: "And it came to pass, when He was in a certain city, behold a man full of leprosy, who seeing Jesus, and falling on his face, besought Him, saying: Lord, if Thou wilt, Thou canst make me clean.

"And stretching forth His hand, He touched him, saying: I will. Be thou cleansed. And immediately the leprosy departed from him.

"And He charged him that he should tell no man, but Go, show thyself to the priest, and offer for thy cleansing according as Moses commanded, for a testimony to them." (St. Luke v, 12–14.)

THE JOURNEYS OF JESUS

This miracle of Our Lord has always been looked upon in the Church as a type of the Sacrament of Penance; for as Our Lord cleansed the afflicted man of the leprosy of the body, so does the Sacrament of Penance cleanse us of sin, the more deadly leprosy of the soul.

Although warned by Jesus to tell no one, the man miraculously cured was so overjoyed that he could not keep the news to himself, but began to tell people, everywhere he went, of the great cure which Jesus had performed. After this, "great multitudes came together to hear, and to be healed by Him of their infirmities. And He retired into the desert, and prayed." (St. Luke v, 15–16.)

QUESTIONS

1. What reason did many of the people have for coming to Jesus?

2. Where did they find Him?

3. For what purpose did Jesus say He was sent?

4. Upon what mission did Jesus go to Capharnaum?

5. After preaching, Jesus usually performed miracles. Why?

6. Tell one thing that happened during the mission through the cities and towns of Galilee.

7. Why was the heart of Jesus moved at the prayer of the leper?

8. What two commands did Jesus give to the leper?

VIII

JESUS IN THE SYNAGOGUE AT CAPHARNAUM

He Cures a Man with an Unclean Spirit

On His return to Capharnaum Jesus went into the synagogue and taught the people. "And they were astonished at His doctrine," says St. Luke (iv, 32), "for His speech was with power."

Not only did He show His power by His words, but also by His miracles. "And in the synagogue there was a man who had an unclean devil, and he cried out with a loud voice,

"Saying: Let us alone, what have we to do with Thee, Jesus of Nazareth? art Thou come to destroy us? I know Thee Who Thou art, the Holy One of God.

"And Jesus rebuked him, saying: Hold thy peace and go out of him. And when the devil had thrown him into the midst, he went out of him, and hurt him not at all.

"And there came fear upon all, and they talked among themselves saying: What word is this, for with authority and power He commandeth the unclean spirits, and they go out?"

The news of such wonders as this could not be kept hidden. "And the fame of Him was published into every place of the country." (St. Luke iv, 33–37.)

QUESTIONS

1. Where did Jesus cure the man with an unclean spirit?

2. In what words did the unclean spirit, when leaving the man, prove that Jesus is God?

JESUS CURES SIMON'S MOTHER-IN-LAW

After the cure of the man with the unclean spirit, Jesus "rising up out of the synagogue, went into Simon's house."

When Our Lord entered He saw Simon's wife's mother, who was suffering from a great fever. Remembering the miracle of healing that they had just seen, the disciples asked Our Lord to relieve the poor sufferer who lay before Him. "And standing over her, He commanded the fever, and it left her. And immediately rising, she ministered to them." (St. Luke iv, 39.)

All sorts of people were interested in Our Lord's miracles of healing, but the sick were especially so.

And we may be sure that, in the families where there were sick persons, there was much talk about Our Lord and His miraculous power.

St. Luke says (iv, 40–41): "And when the sun was down, all they that had any sick with divers diseases, brought them to Him. But He laying His hands on every one of them, healed them.

"And devils went out from many, crying out and saying: Thou art the Son of God. And rebuking them He suffered them not to speak, for they knew that He was Christ."

Cured of their diseases, some of the people that had been healed returned to their homes, but many still wished to be near this great Wonder-Worker, this Prophet who was so full of pity for the sick and the poor. The Gospel says: "And when it was day, going out He went into a desert place, and the multitudes sought Him, and came unto Him: and they stayed Him that He should not depart from them.

"To whom He said: To other cities also I must preach the Kingdom of God: for therefore am I sent.

"And He was preaching in the synagogues of Galilee." (St. Luke iv, 42–44.)

THE JOURNEYS OF JESUS

QUESTIONS

1. While Jesus was in Capharnaum, in whose house did He live?

2. Who else, besides Jesus and His Apostles, lived in the house?

3. How did Jesus show His power in this house?

4. How did the devils, driven out by Jesus, help to make Him better known?

5. Did Jesus care for the praise of men? Prove your answer to this question.

A Synagogue

The word *synagogue* has two meanings. It may mean a congregation. It may also mean the building in which a Jewish congregation gathers. In Our Lord's day there seems to have been a synagogue in every town of any size. It was not intended as a place of sacrifice, but as a school where scriptural instruction was given, and as a place for public prayer.

Its officers were the Ancients, who had general charge of religious matters; the Rulers, whose office was to care for public worship; the Receivers of Alms, who received the gifts and gave them to the needy; and the Minister, or servant, who had the care of the Holy Scriptures, bringing them forth for public worship and putting them away afterwards.

JESUS IN THE SYNAGOGUE AT CAPHARNAUM

In those days books were not printed, but were written on strips of sheepskin which were wrapped around rollers the way we roll big maps in school. Each book of the Scriptures was on a separate strip of sheepskin and was rolled up by itself.

Besides these officers, there were ten men who had always to be present on every occasion of public worship and who received a fee for their services.

QUESTIONS

1. For what purposes were the synagogues used in Our Lord's day?

2. On what was the Law written?

3. Who were the officers in the synagogues?

4. What were their duties?

CHRIST HEALETH THE MAN AFFLICTED WITH THE PALSY

IX

JESUS TEACHES AT CAPHARNAUM

JESUS HEALS A MAN SICK WITH THE PALSY

One day not long after the cure of the leper, Our Lord sat teaching in a certain house. Such a crowd came to hear Him that the house was full. Four men brought another man, who had the palsy, to be cured, carrying him on a bed, or stretcher. The crowd was so great that they could not enter the house. St. Luke (v, 18–19) tells us "they sought means to bring him in, and to lay him before Him. And when they could not find by what way they might bring him in, because of the multitude, they went up upon the roof, and let him down through the tiles with his bed into the midst before Jesus."

When Jesus saw the faith of the sick man, He said to him: "Man, thy sins are forgiven thee.

"And the Scribes and Pharisees began to think, saying: Who is this who speaketh blasphemies? Who can forgive sins, but God alone?

"And when Jesus knew their thoughts, answering, He said to them: What is it you think in your hearts?

"Which is easier to say, Thy sins are forgiven thee; or to say, Arise and walk?

"But that you may know that the Son of Man hath power on earth to forgive sins, (He saith to the sick of the palsy,) I say to thee, Arise, take up thy bed, and go into thy house.

"And immediately rising up before them, he took up the bed on which he lay; and he went away to his own house, glorifying God.

"And all were astonished; and they glorified God. And they were filled with fear, saying: We have seen wonderful things to day." (St. Luke v, 20–26.)

QUESTIONS

1. Tell the story of the man sick with the palsy.

2. What moved Jesus to take pity on this man and cure him?

3. How could Jesus know the thoughts of the Pharisees?

4. Who has power to forgive sins?

5. What does your catechism tell you of the dispositions necessary to obtain pardon for sins?

THE PHARISEES

The Pharisees were Jews who were very particular in their obedience to the Jewish laws and traditions. We know from what Our Lord said to them that they gave more attention to ceremonies than to keeping their hearts holy and humble. They were very scornful of other Jews who were not so careful about religious ceremonies, and they would have nothing to do with Gentiles, or people who were not Jews.

THE SCRIBES

The doctors, or the Scribes, were men who explained to the Jews what the Law meant. When the Scribes taught in public, they sat on benches raised above the listeners. Their disciples sat at their feet, on the floor.

THE SADDUCEES

The Sadducees were mostly the rich and noble men among the Jews. They did not believe that there was any life after this, and in this world they lived a life of enjoyment and ease. The Sadducees did not really care very much for religion. In this they differed from the Pharisees, who cared too much for religious forms and not enough for the spirit of religion.

X

JESUS CALLS LEVI TO FOLLOW HIM

The great roads from Damascus, Tyre, Sephoris, and Jerusalem all met at Capharnaum. In the Roman customhouse there, men who knew the language and habits of the traders and merchants collected the duty, or tax, on the goods that passed through Capharnaum. These collectors, or publicans, were very strict and sometimes even cruel and unjust in their methods. Because of this hard-heartedness and because some of them grew rich by dishonesty they were hated by the ordinary people. When they happened to be Jews, which was often the case, they were especially disliked and were looked upon as traitors to their country and to their religion.

It was from this hated class that Jesus chose his seventh Apostle. St. Luke says (v, 27–28): "And after these things He went forth, and saw a publican named Levi, sitting at the receipt of custom, and He said to him: Follow Me.

"And leaving all things, he rose up and followed Him."

Levi answered the call of the Saviour, and was

never again to be separated from Him. It is likely that it was in grateful remembrance of this call of grace that Levi changed his name to Matthew, "Gift of God," by which name he is known in the Church. We shall read later how Matthew gave a great feast to celebrate his conversion.

QUESTIONS

1. On your map locate the four great roads that met at Capharnaum.

2. Point out Damascus and Jerusalem on the map.

3. What was the chief work of the people who lived in Capharnaum?

4. Give the name of one man mentioned in the Gospel who lived in this city.

5. How did the people feel toward the tax gatherers?

6. Was Jesus particularly interested in any of them?

7. Find out all you can about the publican, Levi.

PART III. THE SECOND YEAR
OF THE PUBLIC MINISTRY OF JESUS

A THIRD JOURNEY
OF JESUS

After the call of Levi, Jesus left Capharnaum and traveled to Jerusalem. He then returned northward and visited the cities and towns of Galilee a second time, returning to Capharnaum. After that he returned to the Lake of Genesareth and went to the Mount of Beatitudes. At the conclusion of His Sermon on the Mount He returned to Capharnaum, going from there to the town of Naim. From Naim he started on a second mission through the land of Galilee. Coming back to the Lake of Genesareth, he spoke in parables concerning the Kingdom of Heaven.

The principal things to be remembered about this journey are:

The Cure of the Man Sick Thirty-eight Years
The Defense of His Disciples against the Pharisees
The Healing of the Withered Hand
The Choosing of the Twelve Apostles
The Sermon on the Mount
The Healing of the Centurion's Servant
The Widow's Son Restored to Life
The Praise of John the Baptist

THE JOURNEYS OF JESUS

The Banquet of Simon the Pharisee
The Defense of Mary Magdalen
Teaching and Healing the Sick through Galilee
The Lake Sermon in Seven Parables:
> The Sower
> The Cockle
> The Mustard Seed
> The Leaven
> The Hidden Treasure
> The Pearl of Great Price
> The Net

Christ's Reason for Speaking in Parables

I

JESUS IN JERUSALEM

JESUS HEALS ON THE SABBATH DAY

About this time the Saviour decided to go up to Jerusalem for the approaching festival season. The Gospel does not mention the name of this celebration, but the most ancient Fathers of the Church looked upon it as the second Passover during the public ministry of Jesus. St. John (v, 2–18) tells of a great cure which Jesus performed at the Holy City.

"Now there is at Jerusalem a pond, called Probatica, which in Hebrew is named Bethsaida, having five porches.

"In these lay a great multitude of sick, of blind, of lame, of withered; waiting for the moving of the water.

"And an angel of the Lord descended at certain times into the pond; and the water was moved. And he that went down first into the pond after the motion of the water, was made whole, of whatsoever infirmity he lay under.

[103]

"And there was a certain man there, that had been eight and thirty years under his infirmity.

"Him when Jesus had seen lying, and knew that he had been now a long time, He saith to him: Wilt thou be made whole?

"The infirm man answered him: Sir, I have no man, when the water is troubled, to put me into the pond. For whilst I am coming, another goeth down before me.

"Jesus saith to him: Arise, take up thy bed, and walk.

"And immediately the man was made whole: and he took up his bed, and walked. And it was the Sabbath that day.

"The Jews therefore said to him that was healed: It is the Sabbath; it is not lawful for thee to take up thy bed.

"He answered them: He that made me whole, He said to me, Take up thy bed, and walk.

"They asked him therefore: Who is that man who said to thee, Take up thy bed, and walk?

"But he who was healed, knew not who it was; for Jesus went aside from the multitude standing in the place.

"Afterwards, Jesus findeth him in the Temple, and saith to him: Behold thou art made whole: sin no more, lest some worse thing happen to thee.

JESUS IN JERUSALEM

"The man went his way, and told the Jews, that it was Jesus who had made him whole.

"Therefore did the Jews persecute Jesus, because He did these things on the Sabbath.

"But Jesus answered them: My Father worketh until now; and I work.

"Hereupon therefore the Jews sought the more to kill Him, because He did not only break the Sabbath, but also said God was His Father, making Himself equal to God."

QUESTIONS

1. Where is the Pool of Bethsaida?

2. Tell of the cure that Jesus performed there.

3. Upon what two occasions did Jesus say "Arise, take up thy bed, and walk"?

4. What two charges were brought against Jesus at the Feast of the Pasch?

5. How did Jesus prove that He is God?

II

JESUS ON THE ROAD TO GALILEE

A Sabbath Walk through the Cornfield

Soon after this, on another Sabbath day, Jesus and His disciples were returning to Galilee. The pathway led through a cornfield—what we should call a wheat field. The disciples were hungry. When they saw the ripe ears of the wheat, they plucked some and ate the grain.

According to Jewish Law harvesting was forbidden on the Sabbath. The Pharisees, who were very strict about the Law, pretended that this plucking of a few ears of wheat was like harvesting a whole crop. So they complained to Our Lord: "Behold Thy disciples do that which is not lawful on the Sabbath days.

"But He said to them: Have you not read what David did when he was hungry, and they that were with him:

"How he entered into the House of God, and did eat the loaves of proposition, which it was not lawful for him to eat, nor for them that were with him, but for the priests only?

[106]

JESUS ON THE ROAD TO GALILEE

"Or have ye not read in the Law, that on the Sabbath days the priests in the Temple break the Sabbath, and are without blame?

"But I tell you that there is here a greater than the Temple.

"And if you knew what this meaneth: *I will have mercy, and not sacrifice*: you would never have condemned the innocent.

"For the Son of Man is Lord even of the Sabbath." (St. Matthew xii, 1–8.)

QUESTIONS

1. Tell what the Apostles did on the way through the Galilean cornfield.

2. What was this corn like?

3. Tell what you know of David and his companions when they were in great need of food.

4. Are servile works ever allowed on the Sabbath day?

5. How did Jesus defend His disciples?

THE BREAD OF PROPOSITION

The bread of proposition was twelve unleavened loaves covered with frankincense, representing the Twelve Tribes of Israel. The loaves were placed, in order, upon a table of precious wood set in the holy place of the Temple.

Each Sabbath the priests came to put fresh loaves in the place of those which had remained all week in the presence of the Lord. The frankincense was burned when the bread on which it had stood was removed. The bread could be touched and eaten in the holy place only by the priests.

It was this sacred bread that David ate when, in the time of the high priest Abiathar, he entered the House of the Lord in great need of food.

III

JESUS IN CAPHARNAUM

The Withered Hand

"And it came to pass also on another Sabbath, that He entered into the synagogue, and taught. And there was a man, whose right hand was withered.

"And the Scribes and Pharisees watched if He would heal on the Sabbath; that they might find an accusation against Him.

"But He knew their thoughts; and said to the man who had the withered hand: Arise, and stand forth in the midst. And rising he stood forth.

"Then Jesus said to them: I ask you, if it be lawful on the Sabbath days to do good, or to do evil; to save life, or to destroy?

"And looking round about on them all, He said to the man: Stretch forth thy hand. And he stretched it forth: and his hand was restored." (St. Luke vi, 6–10.)

Jesus, with a sentence, cured the withered limb. Would they dare to say He had broken the Sabbath?

"And the Pharisees going out made a consultation against Him, how they might destroy Him.

CHRIST HEALETH THE MAN WITH THE WITHERED HAND

JESUS IN CAPHARNAUM

"But Jesus knowing it, retired from thence: and many followed Him, and He healed them all.

"And He charged them that they should not make Him known." (St. Matthew xii, 14–16.)

QUESTIONS

1. Christ said to the man with a withered hand, "Stretch forth thy hand." Did the miracle take place before or after these words of Jesus?

2. Why did the Pharisees consult together to find a way to destroy Jesus?

3. What did Jesus do for the people who followed Him after this miracle?

IV

JESUS ON THE MOUNT

Jesus Chooses the Twelve Apostles

After the Saviour had visited all the places along the western shore of Lake Genesareth, "He went out into a mountain to pray, and He passed the whole night in the prayer of God." (St. Luke vi, 12.)

In the dawning light of the morning after this long prayer, Jesus, as we are told by St. Luke (vi, 13–16), called to Him His disciples, "and He chose twelve of them (whom also He named Apostles): Simon, whom He surnamed Peter, and Andrew his brother, James and John, Philip and Bartholomew,

"Matthew and Thomas, James the son of Alpheus, and Simon who is called Zelotes,

"And Jude, the brother of James, and Judas Iscariot, who was the traitor."

Of the twelve Apostles, seven had been chosen already. These were Peter and Andrew, the sons of Jona; James and John, the sons of Zebedee, and Philip, all from Bethsaida; Bartholomew from Cana in Galilee; and Matthew the publican.

JESUS ON THE MOUNT

At this time Jesus added five others: His two cousins, James the Less and Jude (sometimes called Thaddeus) ; Thomas and Simon the Zealot, both from Galilee; and, last of all, Judas the man from Kerioth in Judea.

St. Matthew (x, 2–4) groups the names of the twelve Apostles two by two in this way: "The first, Simon who is called Peter, and Andrew his brother,

"James the son of Zebedee, and John his brother, Philip and Bartholomew, Thomas and Matthew the publican, and James the son of Alpheus, and Thaddeus;

"Simon the Cananean, and Judas Iscariot, who also betrayed Him."

Simon Peter is named first in all the Gospels, not because he was called first, since his brother Andrew had been called before him, but because from the first Jesus preferred him.

These Apostles, chosen by our Divine Lord, were like twelve precious stones gathered from the dark quarries of the earth. They needed to be cut and polished by the Master's hand before they were set to shine before men and ready to carry the Word to the nations of the earth. The Divine Master Who chose them from the rest of mankind would, during the months that followed, brighten their minds, polish their rude ways, soften their harshness, and fit them to be worthy of carrying on His work on earth. They were the links between the Old and the New Covenant. With the choosing of the Twelve the Catholic Church began its work, which shall last till the end of time.

QUESTIONS

1. Where did the last choice of the Apostles take place?

2. Name an instance when Jesus spent a night in prayer.

3. Who were the first Bishops of the Church?

4. Can you name them?

5. How many of them were from Galilee?

6. Which one was from Judea, where Jesus was born?

7. What lesson did the Saviour give us before He chose His Apostles?

THE SERMON ON THE MOUNT

After choosing the twelve Apostles, Jesus came down with them to the open plain; but seeing the great multitudes assembled, He again ascended the hill now known as the Mount of Beatitudes.

St. Matthew (iv, 25) states that "much people followed Him from Galilee, and from Decapolis, and from Jerusalem, and from Judea, and from beyond the Jordan." And St. Luke (vi, 17) says that there were present "a very great multitude of people from

THE SERMON ON THE MOUNT

all Judea and Jerusalem, and the sea coast both of Tyre and Sidon."

"And when He was set down," says St. Matthew (v, 1–10), "His disciples came unto Him.

"And opening His mouth, He taught them, saying:

"Blessed are the poor in spirit: for theirs is the Kingdom of Heaven.

"Blessed are the meek: for they shall possess the land.

"Blessed are they that mourn: for they shall be comforted.

"Blessed are they that hunger and thirst after justice: for they shall have their fill.

"Blessed are the merciful: for they shall obtain mercy.

"Blessed are the clean of heart: for they shall see God.

"Blessed are the peacemakers: for they shall be called the children of God.

"Blessed are they that suffer persecution for justice' sake: for theirs is the Kingdom of Heaven."

Such was the beginning of the Sermon on the Mount. These eight sentences are called the Eight Beatitudes. They are like eight golden steps, by climbing which we may surely arrive at the blessed home of Our Father in Heaven.

Continuing His sermon, and speaking these words

more especially to His Apostles, Jesus said: "Blessed are ye when they shall revile you, and persecute you, and speak all that is evil against you, untruly, for My sake:

"Be glad and rejoice, for your reward is very great in heaven. For so they persecuted the prophets that were before you.

"You are the salt of the earth. But if the salt lose its savor, wherewith shall it be salted? It is good for nothing any more but to be cast out, and to be trodden on by men.

"You are the light of the world. A city seated on a mountain cannot be hid.

"Neither do men light a candle and put it under a bushel, but upon a candlestick, that it may shine to all that are in the house.

"So let your light shine before men, that they may see your good works, and glorify your Father Who is in heaven.

"Do not think that I am come to destroy the Law, or the Prophets. I am not come to destroy, but to fulfil.

"For amen I say unto you, till heaven and earth pass, one jot, or one tittle shall not pass of the Law, till all be fulfilled.

"He therefore that shall break one of these least commandments, and shall so teach men, shall be called the least in the Kingdom of Heaven. But he that shall do and teach, he shall be called great in the Kingdom of Heaven.

"For I tell you, that unless your justice abound more than that of the Scribes and Pharisees, you shall not enter into the Kingdom of Heaven." (St. Matthew v, 11–20.)

THE MOUNT OF BEATITUDES

A mountain which lies to the left of the principal road leading from Mount Thabor to the Sea of Genesareth is called by Christians the Mount of Beatitudes. This mountain has two peaks. The Arabs call the peaks the Horns of Hattin. They rise about eighteen hundred feet above the level of the Sea of Genesareth.

This is believed to be the hilly country to which the "very great multitude" followed Jesus.

QUESTIONS

1. Where is the Mount of Beatitudes?

2. What two events took place on this mountain?

3. Locate the places from which people came to hear the Sermon on the Mount.

4. Can you give the first part of the Sermon from memory? If so, write it.

JESUS ON THE MOUNT

Jesus Teaches the Necessity of Prayer

Prayer is necessary if we would lead good lives. Our Blessed Lord taught the people how to pray so as to merit God's grace. He said: "And when ye pray, you shall not be as the hypocrites, that love to stand and pray in the synagogues and corners of the streets, that they may be seen by men: Amen I say to you, they have received their reward.

"But thou when thou shalt pray, enter into thy chamber, and having shut the door, pray to thy Father in secret: and thy Father who seeth in secret will repay thee.

"And when you are praying, speak not much, as the heathens. For they think that in their much speaking they may be heard.

"Be not you therefore like to them, for your Father knoweth what is needful for you, before you ask Him.

"Thus therefore shall you pray: Our Father Who Art in heaven, hallowed be Thy Name.

"Thy Kingdom come. Thy will be done on earth as it is in heaven.

"Give us this day our supersubstantial bread.

"And forgive us our debts, as we also forgive our debtors.

"And lead us not into temptation. But deliver us from evil. Amen.

[119]

"For if you will forgive men their offences, your heavenly Father will forgive you also your offences.

"But if you will not forgive men, neither will your Father forgive you your offences." (St. Matthew vi, 5–15.)

SUFFICIENT FOR THE DAY

Then Our Lord warned those who think more of earthly than of heavenly things. He said: "Therefore I say to you, be not solicitous for your life, what you shall eat, nor for your body, what you shall put on. Is not the life more than the meat: and the body more than the raiment?

"Behold the birds of the air, for they neither sow, nor do they reap, nor gather into barns: and your heavenly Father feedeth them. Are not you of much more value than they?

"And which of you by taking thought, can add to his stature one cubit?

"And for raiment why are you solicitous? Consider the lilies of the field, how they grow: They labor not, neither do they spin.

"But I say to you, that not even Solomon in all his glory was arrayed as one of these.

"And if the grass of the field, which is to day and to morrow is cast into the oven, God doth so clothe: how much more you, O ye of little faith?

"Be not solicitous therefore, saying: What shall we eat: or what shall we drink, or wherewith shall we be clothed?

"For after all these things do the heathen seek. For your Father knoweth that you have need of all these things.

"Seek ye therefore first the Kingdom of God, and His justice, and all these things shall be added unto you.

"Be not therefore solicitous for to morrow; for the morrow will be solicitous for itself. Sufficient for the day is the evil thereof." (St. Matthew vi, 25–34.)

Love your Enemies

The Jewish doctors looked upon every foreigner as an enemy, and had no pity upon Gentiles. They taught that the pagan was not a neighbor. In the course of His Sermon on the Mount, we are told by St. Matthew (v, 43–48) that Jesus taught love of all mankind, for God is the Father of all.

Our Lord said: "You have heard that it hath been said, Thou shalt love thy neighbor, and hate thy enemy.

"But I say to you, Love your enemies: do good to them that hate you: and pray for them that persecute and calumniate you:

"That you may be the children of your Father Who is in heaven, Who maketh His sun to rise upon the good, and bad, and raineth upon the just and the unjust.

"For if you love them that love you, what reward shall you have? do not even the publicans this?

"And if you salute your brethren only, what do you more? do not also the heathens this?

"Be you therefore perfect, as also your heavenly Father is perfect."

A House Built upon a Rock

Jesus ended His Sermon on the Mount by inviting all to come to Him. Then He said: "Every one that cometh to Me, and heareth My words, and doth them, I will show you to whom he is like.

"He is like to a man building a house, who digged deep, and laid the foundation upon a rock. And when a flood came, the stream beat vehemently upon that house, and it could not shake it; for it was founded on a rock.

"But he that heareth, and doth not, is like to a man building his house upon the earth without a foundation: against which the stream beat vehemently, and immediately it fell, and the ruin of that house was great." (St. Luke vi, 47–49.)

JESUS ON THE MOUNT

QUESTIONS

1. Can you quote some words of the Sermon on the Mount, besides those that are known as the Beatitudes?

2. To what does Our Lord liken a man who hears and obeys His teaching?

3. What reward will He give to those who teach His words to others?

4. What are Christ's words on brotherly love?

THE CENTURION

V

JESUS IN CAPHARNAUM

Jesus Heals the Centurion's Servant

When the last words of the Sermon on the Mount had been spoken, Jesus came down the mountain slope. He was surrounded by a great multitude, who followed Him into Capharnaum. What happened there is told, as follows, by St. Luke (vii, 2–10).

"And the servant of a certain centurion, who was dear to him, being sick, was ready to die.

"And when he had heard of Jesus, he sent unto Him the ancients of the Jews, desiring Him to come and heal his servant.

"And when they came to Jesus, they besought Him earnestly, saying to Him: He is worthy that Thou shouldst do this for him.

"For he loveth our nation; and he hath built us a synagogue.

"And Jesus went with them. And when He was now not far from the house, the centurion sent his friends to Him, saying: Lord, trouble not Thyself; for I am not worthy that Thou shouldest enter under my roof.

"For which cause neither did I think myself worthy to come to Thee; but say the word, and my servant shall be healed.

"For I also am a man subject to authority, having under me soldiers: and I say to one, Go, and he goeth; and to another, Come, and he cometh; and to my servant, Do this, and he doth it.

"Which Jesus hearing, marvelled: and turning about to the multitude that followed Him, He said: Amen I say to you, I have not found so great faith, not even in Israel.

"And they who were sent, being returned to the house, found the servant whole who had been sick."

This centurion's words have not been forgotten by Christians, for they are repeated in every Mass when the priest says aloud, "*Domine, non sum dignus*," and they are said in secret by every Catholic who humbly draws near to the Table, where Jesus gives Himself to be our Bread of Life.

THE CENTURION

A centurion was an officer in the Roman army. The Roman army was divided into legions. These, in turn, were made up of cohorts, maniples, and centuries. A century was similar to a company in our army. It was supposed to contain a hundred soldiers; and it was commanded by a centurion, or, as we should call him, a captain.

This centurion's care for his servant in illness was unusual in those days. He was a pagan, but his generosity in building a synagogue for the Jews shows that he was a good man, who had respect for religion.

QUESTIONS

1. What was a centurion?

2. Where did the cure of the centurion's servant take place?

3. "I have not found so great faith, not even in Israel." Whose faith is meant?

4. What difference do you notice between the faith of the centurion and that of the ruler whose child Jesus healed?

5. Which one was a Jew? Which one was a Gentile?

6. Finish this speech: "Lord, I am not worthy . . . "

7. What great lesson did Jesus teach by curing the centurion's servant?

8. Quote the words of the ruler to Jesus.

9. Quote the words of the centurion to Jesus.

VI

JESUS AT THE TOWN OF NAIM

THE WIDOW'S SON RESTORED TO LIFE

On the day after the cure of the centurion's servant Our Saviour, with His Apostles and a great multitude, left Capharnaum and traveled southwestward. They came to a little town called Naim, where they met a funeral procession.

"And when He came nigh to the gate of the city, behold a dead man was carried out, the only son of his mother; and she was a widow: and a great multitude of the city was with her.

"Whom when the Lord had seen, being moved with mercy towards her, He said to her: Weep not.

"And He came near and touched the bier. And they that carried it, stood still. And He said: Young man, I say to thee, arise.

"And he that was dead, sat up, and began to speak. And He gave him to his mother.

"And there came a fear on them all: and they glorified God, saying: A great prophet is risen up among us: and, God hath visited His people.

[128]

CHRIST RAISETH THE WIDOW'S SON

THE JOURNEYS OF JESUS

"And this rumour of Him went forth throughout all Judea, and throughout all the country round about." (St. Luke vii, 12–17.)

QUESTIONS

1. Locate Naim on your map.

2. How did Jesus, at His entrance into Naim, prove Himself to be Master of life and death?

3. How did this miracle affect those who saw it?

4. How did it happen that there were so many people at this funeral?

5. Find in the Bible what you can of the Prophet Eliseus.

6. Near this city of Naim, Eliseus raised to life the son of the Sunamite. Compare how he did so with the way in which Jesus raised to life the son of the widow of Naim.

7. Quote the words of the people when Jesus raised the young man of Naim to life.

8. This is the second person whom Jesus raised to life. Who was the first?

NAIM

Naim was a little town or village about twenty-five miles southwest of Capharnaum. Today it is only a miserable little village of poor people who live in hovels. In the village there is a chapel which was built by the Franciscans in 1880.

JESUS AT THE TOWN OF NAIM

EASTERN BURIALS

Eastern towns and cities at the time of Christ were walled in for protection against enemies. Jews, Romans, and Greeks buried their dead outside the city gates. The dead were carried on biers to the grave. A bier was an open coffin, rather like a plank with handles at each end for the carriers. The corpse was covered with a cloth. Burial followed almost immediately after death. Custom required that whoever saw a funeral procession should follow it and go with the mourners to the grave.

JOHN THE BAPTIST SENDS MESSENGERS TO JESUS

Some of John's disciples were among those that saw Jesus raise the young man of Naim from the dead. They were still full of wonder over this great miracle when they next visited John and "told him of all these things."

"And John called to him two of his disciples, and sent them to Jesus, saying: Art Thou He that art to come; or look we for another?

"And when the men were come unto Him, they said: John the Baptist hath sent us to Thee, saying: Art Thou He that art to come; or look we for another?

[131]

THE JOURNEYS OF JESUS

("And in that same hour, He cured many of their diseases, and hurts, and evil spirits: and to many that were blind He gave sight.)

"And answering, He said to them: Go and relate to John what you have heard and seen: the blind see, the lame walk, the lepers are made clean, the deaf hear, the dead rise again, to the poor the Gospel is preached:

"And blessed is he whosoever that shall not be scandalized in Me." (St. Luke vii, 18–23.)

John's disciples left Jesus and returned to John, who rejoiced at all the things they related to him of the works of Jesus.

Jesus Praises John the Baptist

"And when the messengers of John were departed, He began to speak to the multitudes concerning John. What went ye out into the desert to see? a reed shaken in the wind?

"But what went ye out to see? a man clothed in soft garments? Behold they that are in costly apparel and live delicately, are in the houses of kings.

"But what went you out to see? a prophet? Yea, I say to you, and more than a prophet.

"This is he of whom it is written: *Behold I send my angel before Thy face, who shall prepare Thy way before Thee.*

JESUS AT THE TOWN OF NAIM

"For I say to you: Amongst those that are born of women, there is not a greater prophet than John the Baptist. But he that is the lesser in the Kingdom of God, is greater than he.

"And all the people hearing, and the publicans, justified God, being baptized with John's baptism.

"But the Pharisees and the lawyers despised the counsel of God against themselves, being not baptized by him.

"And the Lord said: Whereunto then shall I liken the men of this generation? and to what are they like?

"They are like to children sitting in the market-place and speaking one to another, and saying: We have piped to you, and you have not danced: we have mourned, and you have not wept.

"For John the Baptist came neither eating bread nor drinking wine; and you say: He hath a devil.

"The Son of Man is come eating and drinking: and you say: Behold a man that is a glutton and a drinker of wine, a friend of publicans and sinners.

"And wisdom is justified by all her children." (St. Luke vii, 24–35.)

QUESTIONS

1. Jesus praised John the Baptist. Which of His words do you think gives John the greatest honor?

2. What is a prophet?

3. Jesus said John was "more than a prophet." In what way was he greater?

4. On this occasion to what did Jesus compare the Pharisees?

THE PHARISEE'S BANQUET

The very day that Jesus raised from the dead the son of the widow of Naim, one of the Pharisees, named Simon, desired Him to eat with him. What happened at the meal is told by St. Luke (vii, 37–50).

"And behold a woman that was in the city, a sinner, when she knew that He sat at meat in the Pharisee's house, brought an alabaster box of ointment;

"And standing behind at His feet, she began to wash His feet, with tears, and wiped them with the hairs of her head, and kissed His feet, and anointed them with the ointment.

"And the Pharisee, who had invited Him, seeing it, spoke within himself, saying: This man, if he were a prophet, would know surely who and what manner of woman this is that toucheth Him, that she is a sinner.

"And Jesus answering, said to him: Simon, I have somewhat to say to thee. But he said: Master, say it.

"A certain creditor had two debtors, the one owed five hundred pence, and the other fifty.

[134]

JESUS AT THE TOWN OF NAIM

"And whereas they had not wherewith to pay, he forgave them both. Which therefore of the two loveth him most?

"Simon answering, said: I suppose that he to whom he forgave most. And He said to him: Thou hast judged rightly.

"And turning to the woman, He said unto Simon: Dost thou see this woman? I entered into thy house, thou gavest me no water for my feet; but she with tears hath washed my feet, and with her hairs hath wiped them.

"Thou gavest me no kiss; but she, since she came in, hath not ceased to kiss my feet.

"My head with oil thou didst not anoint; but she with ointment hath anointed my feet.

"Wherefore I say to thee: Many sins are forgiven her, because she hath loved much. But to whom less is forgiven, he loveth less.

"And He said to her: Thy sins are forgiven thee.

"And they that sat at meat with Him began to say within themselves: Who is This that forgiveth sins also?

"And He said to the woman: Thy faith hath made thee safe, go in peace."

THE JOURNEYS OF JESUS

Eastern Customs at Banquets

In Eastern countries it was the custom for a guest to be met by a servant at the door of the house. The servant took off the guest's sandals and left them in the hall. Then the host kissed the cheek of the guest, saying, "Peace be to you," and after that led him to a seat. A servant then came and bathed the feet of the guest in cool, refreshing water, and the host poured perfumed ointment over his hair and beard. The guest washed his hands just before the meal began.

For some reason or other Simon had not offered to Jesus any of these polite marks of respect. Jesus had not made any complaint about this neglect, but had quietly taken His place at the table.

The tables were arranged round three sides of a square. The guests reclined on low couches or cushioned benches placed at the sides of the table; their feet were turned outward from the table, the left arm rested on the cushions, and the right arm was left free to be used in eating. The host sat or reclined at the upper end of the table, and the guest of honor was at his right. When the banquet was ready, the doors were thrown open, and outsiders were free to enter and talk to the invited guests.

MARY MAGDALEN AT THE LORD'S FEET

THE JOURNEYS OF JESUS

Mary Magdalen

St. Luke does not give the name of the sinful woman who washed the feet of Jesus with tears, at Simon's banquet, but it is believed that she was Mary Magdalen. In gratitude for the mercy shown to her then by Our Lord, she became one of His most faithful followers. We find her with the Blessed Virgin and St. John at the foot of the cross on the day of the Crucifixion, and she was the first to whom Our Lord showed Himself after His Resurrection.

QUESTIONS

1. Show how Simon the Pharisee, at his banquet, failed in courtesy to Jesus.

2. Did Simon invite Mary Magdalen to his feast?

3. How did she come to be present?

4. How did Mary, the sinner, act at the banquet?

5. What did Simon think of her?

6. How did Jesus lead Simon to see the evil of his thoughts about Mary Magdalen?

7. What reason did Jesus give for His pardon of all her sins?

8. Jesus did not say to Mary, as He did to others, "Sin no more." Can you think why He did not?

9. Is there any way, other than by the Sacrament of Penance, that grievous sin can be forgiven?

10. Show that Mary Magdalen had a firm purpose of amendment.

11. Was anything more heard of Mary after Simon's banquet?

12. What dispositions on her part made her deserving of forgiveness?

VII

JESUS IN GALILEE

The days which followed the conversion of Mary Magdalen were spent in preaching the Gospel to the people.

"And it came to pass afterwards, that He travelled through the cities and towns, preaching and evangelizing the Kingdom of God; and the Twelve with Him:

"And certain women who had been healed of evil spirits and infirmities; Mary who is called Magdalen, out of whom seven devils were gone forth,

"And Joanna the wife of Chusa, Herod's steward, and Susanna, and many others who ministered unto Him of their substance." (St. Luke viii, 1–3.)

A HOUSE DIVIDED AGAINST ITSELF

"And they come to a house, and the multitude cometh together again, so that they could not so much as eat bread.

[140]

"And when His friends had heard of it, they went out to lay hold on Him. For they said: He is become mad.

"And the Scribes who were come down from Jerusalem, said: He hath Beelzebub, and by the prince of devils he casteth out devils.

"And after He had called them together, He said to them in parables: How can Satan cast out Satan?

"And if a kingdom be divided against itself, that kingdom cannot stand.

"And if a house be divided against itself, that house cannot stand.

"And if Satan be risen up against himself, he is divided, and cannot stand, but hath an end.

"No man can enter into the house of a strong man and rob him of his goods, unless he first bind the strong man, and then shall he plunder his house.

"Amen I say to you, that all sins shall be forgiven unto the sons of men, and the blasphemies wherewith they shall blaspheme:

"But he that shall blaspheme against the Holy Ghost, shall never have forgiveness, but shall be guilty of an everlasting sin.

"Because they said: He hath an unclean spirit.

"And His mother and His brethren came; and standing without, sent unto Him, calling Him.

[141]

THE JOURNEYS OF JESUS

"And the multitude sat about Him; and they say to Him: Behold Thy mother and Thy brethren without seek for Thee.

"And answering them, He said: Who is My mother and My brethren?

"And looking round about on them who sat about Him, He saith: Behold My mother and My brethren.

"For whosoever shall do the will of God, He is My brother, and My sister, and mother." (St. Mark iii, 20–35.)

Then rising, Jesus left the house and took the road leading to the Lake of Genesareth.

QUESTIONS

1. How can we tell that Jesus did not live with His relatives at this time?

2. What is blasphemy?

3. What is meant by "final impenitence"?

4. Is there any sin that shall not be forgiven if the sinner has the proper dispositions?

5. What are the proper dispositions?

6. What do you think is the meaning of a "house divided against itself"?

VIII

THE LAKE SERMON IN SEVEN PARABLES

THE SOWER AND THE COCKLE

Our Lord, as we know, often spoke in parables. These were stories told for the purpose of making plain to the people the truths He was teaching. The parables were about things with which the people were familiar, things of everyday life, such as the sowing of seed, the losing of a piece of money, the straying away of a sheep from the flock, and so forth; and they were intended to teach the people about God's love, or God's justice, or God's mercy.

In one of these parables, given by St. Luke (viii, 5–8), Jesus said: "The sower went out to sow his seed. And as he sowed, some fell by the way side, and it was trodden down, and the fowls of the air devoured it.

"And other some fell upon a rock: and as soon as it was sprung up, it withered away, because it had no moisture.

"And other some fell among thorns, and the thorns growing up with it, choked it.

[143]

JESUS SEATED BY THE SEA SIDE

"And other some fell upon good ground; and being sprung up, yielded fruit a hundredfold. Saying these things, He cried out: He that hath ears to hear, let him hear."

Then Our Saviour told another parable, saying: "The Kingdom of Heaven is likened to a man that sowed good seed in his field.

"But while men were asleep, his enemy came and oversowed cockle among the wheat and went his way.

"And when the blade was sprung up, and had brought forth fruit, then appeared also the cockle.

"And the servants of the goodman of the house coming said to him: Sir, didst thou not sow good seed in thy field? whence then hath it cockle?

"And he said to them: An enemy hath done this. And the servants said to him: Wilt thou that we go and gather it up?

"And he said: No, lest perhaps gathering up the cockle, you root up the wheat also together with it.

"Suffer both to grow until the harvest, and in the time of the harvest I will say to the reapers: Gather up first the cockle, and bind it into bundles to burn, but the wheat gather ye into my barn." (St. Matthew xiii, 24–30.)

Cockle is a weed that fastens itself to the root of the wheat and cannot be told from wheat until the wheat begins to ripen.

[145]

THE JOURNEYS OF JESUS

The Mustard Seed and the Leaven

In the parable of The Sower and the Cockle Our Lord pointed out how the Word of God may be hindered from complete growth by many things. This sometimes happens in the Church or in our souls.

For fear that His disciples should be discouraged at the thought of so many difficulties, Our Lord gave two other parables. These were about the mustard seed and the leaven, which both grow in spite of every hindrance.

St. Matthew tells the parable of the mustard seed: "The Kingdom of Heaven is like to a grain of mustard seed, which a man took and sowed in his field.

"Which is the least indeed of all seeds; but when it is grown up, it is greater than all herbs, and becometh a tree, so that the birds of the air come, and dwell in the branches thereof." (St. Matthew xiii, 31–32.)

The parable of the leaven is the second given by our Divine Saviour to the Apostles to encourage them in their future great labors in the Church. As we read in St. Luke (xiii, 20–21), "Whereunto shall I esteem the Kingdom of God to be like?

"It is like to leaven, which a woman took and hid in three measures of meal, till the whole was leavened."

[146]

THE LAKE SERMON IN SEVEN PARABLES

The Hidden Treasure, The Pearl of Great Price, and The Net

These parables were not spoken to the multitude, but to the disciples, for St. Matthew writes (xiii, 36): "Then having sent away the multitudes, He came into the house, and His disciples came to Him, saying: Expound to us the parable of the cockle of the field."

The Divine Master did as they desired Him, and added these two parables: "The Kingdom of Heaven is like unto a treasure hidden in a field. Which a man having found, hid it, and for joy thereof goeth, and selleth all that he hath, and buyeth that field.

"Again the Kingdom of Heaven is like to a merchant seeking good pearls.

"Who when he had found one pearl of great price, went his way, and sold all that he had, and bought it." (St. Matthew xiii, 45–46.)

In Palestine treasures were often hidden because of so many thefts by enemies. The Jewish law gave to the buyer of the field the treasure found in it.

Our Lord said, also, "The Kingdom of Heaven is like unto a net cast into the sea, and gathering together of all kinds of fishes." (St. Matthew xiii, 47.) By this He meant that the Church is a society wherein are good and bad members, just as there are good and bad fish in the net.

THE JOURNEYS OF JESUS

Jesus' Reason for Speaking in Parables

To the multitudes our Divine Lord spoke in parables, but He made things plain to His own disciples. We are told by St. Matthew (xiii, 10–13) that when the disciples asked Him why He spoke to the people in parables, Our Lord said: "Because to you it is given to know the mysteries of the Kingdom of Heaven: but to them it is not given.

"For he that hath, to him shall be given, and he shall abound: but he that hath not, from him shall be taken away that also which he hath.

"Therefore do I speak to them in parables: because seeing they see not, and hearing they hear not, neither do they understand."

Then He explained the parables to them, and asked: "Have ye understood all these things?" They answered "Yes." Then He said: "Therefore every scribe instructed in the Kingdom of Heaven, is like to a man that is a householder, who bringeth forth out of his treasure new things and old." (St. Matthew xiii, 51–52.)

QUESTIONS

1. Tell why Jesus spoke in parables.

2. To what do all the parables relate?

3. Can you give any reason why Our Saviour gave the parable of the mustard seed?

4. Trace in a very short paragraph how the Church is like the mustard seed.

5. At the present time is anything being done to spread the branches of that Mighty Tree—the Church? If so, tell in what way or ways and where.

6. How can all, even young children, help to spread the Kingdom of God on earth?

7. What are you doing to help this work?

8. To what class of people are the parables of the pearl and the treasure especially addressed?

9. Name four conditions of the soil named in the parable of the sower.

10. The Apostles asked the Master to explain to them the parable of the cockle. Quote His answer to them, if you can.

11. Why are the wicked permitted to live and to annoy the good?

A FOURTH JOURNEY
OF JESUS

In His fourth journey Jesus and His Apostles crossed from Capharnaum, over the Lake of Genesareth, to the land of the Gerasens in the neighborhood of Gadara. From here He recrossed the lake to its western side, landing at the plain of Genesareth near Capharnaum. Then He visited Nazareth for the last time; and for a third time He visited all the cities and towns of Galilee, and returned to Capharnaum.

The principal things to be remembered about this journey are:

The Storm at Sea
The Cure of the Demoniac of Gerasa
The Cure of the Woman with an Issue of Blood
The Daughter of Jairus Raised to Life
The Restoring of Sight to Two Blind Men
The Last Visit to Nazareth
The Third Journey of Jesus through Galilee
The Praise of John the Baptist
The Apostles Sent Out to Preach
The Death of John the Baptist

IX

JESUS IN GERASA AND ON THE LAKE

A GREAT STORM AT SEA

"And He saith to them that day, when evening was come: Let us pass over to the other side.

"And sending away the multitude, they take Him even as He was in the ship: and there were other ships with Him.

"And there arose a great storm of wind, and the waves beat into the ship, so that the ship was filled.

"And He was in the hinder part of the ship, sleeping upon a pillow; and they awake Him, and say to Him: Master, doth it not concern Thee that we perish?

"And rising up, He rebuked the wind, and said to the sea: Peace, be still. And the wind ceased: and there was made a great calm.

"And He said to them: Why are you fearful? have you not faith yet? And they feared exceedingly: and they said, one to another: Who is This (thinkest thou) that both wind and sea obey Him?" (St. Mark iv, 35–40.)

JESUS ASLEEP DURING THE TEMPEST

JESUS IN GERASA AND ON THE LAKE

It is but natural that Catholic writers should find in this incident a type of what one sees in the world today. The Church is the ship, with Christ on board. No matter, therefore, how wild may be the tempest of opposition, we know that we need not fear, since our Divine Lord can and will still that tempest even as He calmed the waves and winds on the Sea of Galilee.

QUESTIONS

1. Of what is the tempest-tossed ship a figure?

2. Why did Jesus rebuke the frightened Apostles?

3. In what virtue did the Apostles at that time seem to be lacking?

4. In what words did the Apostles, after the storm, show admiration for Jesus?

5. In what way did Jesus show His human nature while He was in the ship?

6. In what did He show His divine nature on this same occasion?

JESUS CURES THE DEMONIAC OF GERASA

The next morning the little ship "came over the strait of the sea into the country of the Gerasens.

"And as He went out of the ship, immediately there met Him out of the monuments a man with an unclean spirit, . . .

"And seeing Jesus afar off, he ran and adored Him.

"And crying with a loud voice, he said: What have I to do with Thee, Jesus the Son of the Most High God? I adjure Thee by God that Thou torment me not.

"For He said unto him: Go out of the man, thou unclean spirit.

"And He asked him: What is thy name? And he saith to Him: My name is Legion, for we are many.

"And he besought Him much, that He would not drive him away out of the country.

"And there was there near the mountain a great herd of swine, feeding.

"And the spirits besought Him, saying: Send us into the swine, that we may enter into them.

"And Jesus immediately gave them leave. And the unclean spirits going out, entered into the swine: and the herd with great violence was carried headlong into the sea, being about two thousand, and were stifled in the sea.

"And they that fed them fled, and told it in the city and in the fields. And they went out to see what was done.

"And they came to Jesus, and they see him that was troubled with the devil, sitting, clothed, and well in his wits, and they were afraid.

"And they that had seen it, told them, in what manner he had been dealt with who had the devil; and concerning the swine.

"And they began to pray Him that He would depart from their coasts.

"And when He went up into the ship, he that had been troubled with the devil, began to beseech Him that he might be with Him.

"And He admitted him not, but saith to him: Go into thy house to thy friends, and tell them how great things the Lord hath done for thee, and hath had mercy on thee.

"And he went his way, and began to publish in Decapolis how great things Jesus had done for him: and all men wondered." (St. Mark v, 1–20.)

Jesus thus left in this country a grateful man who became His herald and prepared the hearts of the inhabitants, little by little, to receive His doctrine when He, Himself, should return about a year later.

DECAPOLIS

Decapolis was a union of ten cities in the northeast part of Judea. The country was subject to Rome. The principal city of the union was Scythopolis.

THE JOURNEYS OF JESUS

The Land of the Gerasens

Three names are used for this land "which is over against Galilee." St. Matthew calls the people Gerasens. The country of the Gerasens was thirty-six miles southeast of the Sea, or Lake, of Genesareth.

Gadara was about five miles southeast of the lake, and Gergesa was a few rods from the seashore. A high mountain rises immediately above this sea, and many ancient tombs are in the sides of the mountain.

QUESTIONS

1. Point out on the map the land called Decapolis.

2. In what part of it was the city of Scythopolis?

3. Find on the map the land of the Gerasens.

4. How did the man delivered of the unclean spirit show his gratitude to Jesus?

X

JESUS IN CAPHARNAUM

The Banquet Given by Levi

Jesus left the country of the Gerasens on the same morning that He arrived there. From a distance the ship was seen coming back to Galilee, and a crowd gathered to receive Him. No one was more glad to see Jesus return than Levi (Matthew), who had remained at home to prepare a banquet for Jesus and His friends on their return.

"And it came to pass as He was sitting at meat in the house, behold many publicans and sinners came, and sat down with Jesus and His disciples.

"And the Pharisees seeing it, said to His disciples: Why doth your master eat with publicans and sinners?

"But Jesus hearing it, said: They that are in health need not a physician, but they that are ill.

"Go then and learn what this meaneth, *I will have mercy and not sacrifice*. For I am not come to call the just, but sinners.

"Then came to Him the disciples of John, saying:

[157]

JESUS EATETH WITH PUBLICANS AND SINNERS

Why do we and the Pharisees fast often, but Thy disciples do not fast?

"And Jesus said to them: Can the children of the bridegroom mourn, as long as the bridegroom is with them? But the days will come, when the bridegroom shall be taken away from them, and then they shall fast.

"And nobody putteth a piece of raw cloth unto an old garment. For it taketh away the fulness thereof from the garment, and there is made a greater rent.

"Neither do they put new wine into old bottles. Otherwise the bottles break, and the wine runneth out, and the bottles perish. But new wine they put into new bottles: and both are preserved." (St. Matthew ix, 10–17.)

QUESTIONS

1. Why did Levi give a feast and invite Jesus and His disciples?

2. Who were the publicans?

3. Were any at the feast who were not invited?

4. Why did they come uninvited?

5. What did John the Baptist's disciples ask Jesus?

6. What did Jesus mean by saying "bridegroom" and "the children of the bridegroom"?

7. From what time did the Pharisees and Scribes begin to attack Jesus in public?

THE JOURNEYS OF JESUS

A Girl and a Woman Cured

"And behold there came a man whose name was Jairus, and he was a ruler of the synagogue: and he fell down at the feet of Jesus, beseeching Him that He would come into his house:

"For he had an only daughter, almost twelve years old, and she was dying. And it happened as He went, that He was thronged by the multitudes.

"And there was a certain woman having an issue of blood twelve years, who had bestowed all her substance on physicians, and could not be healed by any.

"She came behind Him, and touched the hem of His garment; and immediately the issue of her blood stopped.

"And Jesus said: Who is it that touched Me? And all denying, Peter and they that were with Him said: Master, the multitudes throng and press Thee, and dost Thou say, Who touched Me?

"And Jesus said: Somebody hath touched Me; for I know that virtue is gone out from Me.

"And the woman seeing that she was not hid, came trembling, and fell down before His feet, and declared before all the people for what cause she had touched Him, and how she was immediately healed.

"But He said to her: Daughter, thy faith hath made thee whole; go thy way in peace.

JESUS HEALETH A WOMAN

THE JOURNEYS OF JESUS

"As He was yet speaking, there cometh one to the ruler of the synagogue, saying to him: Thy daughter is dead, trouble Him not.

"And Jesus hearing this word, answered the father of the maid: Fear not; believe only, and she shall be safe.

"And when He was come to the house, He suffered not any man to go in with Him, but Peter and James and John, and the father and mother of the maiden.

"And all wept and mourned for her. But He said: Weep not; the maid is not dead, but sleepeth.

"And they laughed Him to scorn, knowing that she was dead.

"But He taking her by the hand, cried out, saying: Maid, arise.

"And her spirit returned, and she arose immediately. And He bid them give her to eat.

"And her parents were astonished, whom He charged to tell no man what was done." (St. Luke viii, 41–56.)

QUESTIONS

1. On the way to Jairus's house, what miracle was performed?

2. Can you give any other instances where the faith of a Gentile was stronger than that of a Jew?

3. What virtue does Jesus expect to find in one who asks His favor?

JESUS RAISETH A YOUNG CHILD FROM DEATH

THE JOURNEYS OF JESUS

Public Mourners

The minstrels, or public mourners among the Jews, were either men or women. It was customary to begin the funeral wail immediately after the person's death. The mourning continued eight days. In the case of a king it lasted a month. A similar mourning custom is still observed in Eastern countries, even among Christians.

Sometimes the songs of grief were very beautiful. The beautiful lamentations of David over his friend Jonathan are examples of these mournful dirges, or songs.

From David's Lament for Jonathan

"I grieve for thee, my brother Jonathan: exceeding beautiful, and amiable to me above the love of women. As the mother loveth her only son, so did I love thee." (2 Kings i, 26.)

XI

JESUS ON THE WAY FROM JAIRUS'S HOUSE

Jesus Restores Sight to Two Blind Men

As Our Saviour went from the house of the grateful ruler of the synagogue "there followed Him two blind men crying out and saying, Have mercy on us, O Son of David." This is the first time we hear this title given to Jesus, although it was known to the public that Jesus was a descendant of David.

And when Jesus "was come to the house, the blind men came to Him. And Jesus saith to them, Do you believe, that I can do this unto you? They say to Him, Yea, Lord.

"Then He touched their eyes, saying, According to your faith, be it done unto you.

"And their eyes were opened, and Jesus strictly charged them, saying, See that no man know this.

"But they going out, spread His fame abroad in all that country." (St. Matthew ix, 27–31.)

It was more from an impulsive gratitude than from any ill-will that the two blind men disobeyed the command given them.

THE TWO BLIND MEN OF JERICHO

JESUS ON THE WAY FROM JAIRUS'S HOUSE

QUESTIONS

1. When and where was the title "Son of David" given to Jesus?

2. What was meant by "According to your faith, be it done unto you"?

3. How did the blind men show their gratitude to Jesus?

4. What did they do that teaches us what makes an act good or bad?

XII

JESUS IN NAZARETH

JESUS VISITS NAZARETH FOR THE LAST TIME

"And going from thence, He went into His own country; and His disciples followed Him.

"And when the Sabbath was come He began to teach in the synagogue: and many hearing him were in admiration at His doctrine, saying: How came this Man by all these things? and what wisdom is this that is given to Him, and such mighty works as are wrought by His hands?

"Is not this the carpenter, the son of Mary, the brother of James, and Joseph, and Jude, and Simon? are not also His sisters here with us? And they were scandalized in regard of Him.

"And Jesus said to them: A prophet is not without honor, but in his own country, and in his own house, and among his own kindred.

"And He could not do any miracles there, only that He cured a few . . ., laying His hands upon them.

"And He wondered because of their unbelief, and He went through the villages round about teaching." (St. Mark vi, 1–6.)

JESUS IN NAZARETH

QUESTIONS

1. Who are meant by His brethren and His sisters?
2. Why did the Nazarenes think so little of Jesus?

THE THIRD MISSION OF JESUS THROUGH GALILEE

This is the third time that Jesus makes a missionary trip through Galilee. The first time only a few disciples went with Him, the second time His twelve Apostles and a few of the pious women upon whom He had conferred favors accompanied Him; now on this third journey through Galilee He takes His Apostles and sends them off to preach.

He "went about all the cities, and towns, teaching in their synagogues, and preaching the Gospel of the Kingdom, and healing every disease, and every infirmity.

"And seeing the multitudes, He had compassion on them: because they were distressed, and lying like sheep that have no shepherd."

Jesus saw the willingness of these poor people to receive the Gospel tidings. They were like a field ready for harvest. Jesus said to His disciples: "The harvest indeed is great, but the labourers are few.

"Pray ye therefore the Lord of the harvest, that He send forth labourers into His harvest." (St. Matthew ix, 35–38.)

THE JOURNEYS OF JESUS

QUESTIONS

1. Give the incidents that occurred on Christ's first mission through Galilee.

2. Who were with Him on His second journey through Galilee?

3. What did the Apostles have to do with the third journey through Galilee?

THE MISSION OF THE APOSTLES

"And having called His twelve disciples together, He gave them power over unclean spirits, to cast them out, and to heal all manner of diseases, and all manner of infirmities. . . .

"These twelve Jesus sent: commanding them, saying: Go ye not into the way of the Gentiles, and into the city of the Samaritans enter ye not.

"But go ye rather to the lost sheep of the House of Israel.

"And going, preach, saying: The Kingdom of Heaven is at hand.

"Heal the sick, raise the dead, cleanse the lepers, cast out devils: freely have you received, freely give.

"Do not possess gold, nor silver, nor money in your purses:

"Nor scrip for your journey, nor two coats, nor shoes, nor a staff; for the workman is worthy of his meat.

"And into whatsoever city or town you shall enter, inquire who in it is worthy, and there abide till you go thence.

"And when you come into the house, salute it, saying: Peace be to this house.

"And if that house be worthy, your peace shall come upon it; but if it be not worthy, your peace shall return to you.

"And whosoever shall not receive you, nor hear your words: going forth out of that house or city shake off the dust from your feet.

"Amen I say to you, it shall be more tolerable for the land of Sodom and Gomorrha in the day of judgment, than for that city.

"Behold I send you as sheep in the midst of wolves. Be ye therefore wise as serpents and simple as doves.

"But beware of men. For they will deliver you up in councils, and they will scourge you in their synagogues.

"And you shall be brought before governors, and before kings for My sake, for a testimony to them and to the Gentiles:

"But when they shall deliver you up, take no thought how or what to speak: for it shall be given you in that hour what to speak.

"For it is not you that speak, but the Spirit of your Father that speaketh in you.

"The brother also shall deliver up the brother to death, and the father the son: and the children shall rise up against their parents, and shall put them to death.

"And you shall be hated by all men for My Name's sake: but he that shall persevere unto the end, he shall be saved.

"And when they shall persecute you in this city, flee into another. Amen I say to you, you shall not finish all the cities of Israel, till the Son of Man come.

"The disciple is not above the master, nor the servant above his lord.

"It is enough for the disciple that he be as his master, and the servant as his lord. If they have called the goodman of the house Beelzebub, how much more them of his household?

"Therefore fear them not. For nothing is covered that shall not be revealed: nor hid, that shall not be known.

"That which I tell you in the dark, speak ye in the light: and that which you hear in the ear, preach ye upon the housetops.

"And fear ye not them that kill the body, and are not able to kill the soul: but rather fear Him that can destroy both soul and body in hell.

"Are not two sparrows sold for a farthing? and not one of them shall fall on the ground without your Father.

"Fear not therefore: better are you than many sparrows.

"Every one therefore that shall confess Me before men, I will also confess him before My Father Who is in heaven.

"But he that shall deny Me before men, I will also deny him before My Father Who is in heaven.

"Do not think that I came to send peace upon earth: I came not to send peace, but the sword.

"For I came to set a man at variance against his father, and the daughter against her mother, and the daughter in law against her mother in law.

"And a man's enemies shall be they of his own household.

"He that loveth father or mother more than Me, is not worthy of Me; and he that loveth son or daughter more than Me, is not worthy of Me.

"And he that taketh not up his cross, and followeth Me, is not worthy of Me.

"He that findeth his life, shall lose it: and he that shall lose his life for Me, shall find it.

"He that receiveth you, receiveth Me: and he that receiveth Me, receiveth Him that sent Me.

"He that receiveth a prophet in the name of a prophet, shall receive the reward of a prophet: and he that receiveth a just man in the name of a just man, shall receive the reward of a just man.

BEHEADING OF JOHN THE BAPTIST

JESUS IN NAZARETH

"And whosoever shall give to drink to one of these little ones a cup of cold water only in the name of a disciple, amen I say to you, he shall not lose his reward." (St. Matthew x, 1–42.)

THE DEATH OF JOHN THE BAPTIST

The anniversary of Herod's birthday was celebrated according to heathen customs by a state banquet at which all the princes and chief men of Galilee were gathered. The castle walls were decorated with rich tapestry. The hall was brilliant with lights. There was rich food, music, and dancing.

Salome, a daughter of Herodias, was a graceful dancer. At the party she danced before Herod and those who were at table with him. He was so pleased with her dancing that he bound himself by an oath to give her whatever she might desire, even though it were half the kingdom. Salome went out and said to her mother, "What shall I ask?" The wicked woman told her daughter to ask for the head of John the Baptist. Going back to Herod, this girl without pity or shame said to him, "I will that forthwith thou give me in a dish, the head of John the Baptist.

"And the king was struck sad. Yet because of his oath, and because of them that were with him at table, he would not displease her:

HERODIAS AND THE HEAD OF JOHN THE BAPTIST

"But sending an executioner, he commanded that his head should be brought in a dish.

"And he beheaded him in the prison, and brought his head in a dish: and gave it to the damsel, and the damsel gave it to her mother.

"Which his disciples hearing came, and took his body, and laid it in a tomb." (St. Mark vi, 21–29.)

QUESTIONS

1. In what way had John shown himself to be a man of courage?

2. Was Herod obliged to keep his oath to Salome?

3. When does the Church celebrate the Feast of John the Baptist?

A FIFTH JOURNEY
OF JESUS

After the missionary labors of the Apostles ended they returned to Capharnaum.

From here Jesus invited them to "a desert place" belonging to Bethsaida, on the eastern shore of the lake. From this desert, in the evening after the Miracle of Loaves, Jesus sent the disciples over the lake. Crossing it, they encountered a great storm. Christ came to rejoin them; together they all came again to Capharnaum.

The principal things to be remembered about this short journey are:

> The First Multiplication of Loaves
> The Walking on the Water
> The Promise of the Holy Eucharist
> The Prophecy of Christ's Betrayal

XIII

JESUS IN THE DESERT PLACE NEAR BETHSAIDA-JULIAS

THE FIRST MULTIPLICATION OF LOAVES

"And the Apostles coming together unto Jesus, related to Him all things that they had done and taught.

"And He said to them: Come apart into a desert place, and rest a little. For there were many coming and going: and they had not so much as time to eat.

"And going up into a ship, they went into a desert place apart." (St. Mark vi, 30–32.)

"After these things Jesus went over the sea of Galilee, which is that of Tiberias.

"And a great multitude followed Him, because they saw the miracles which He did on them that were diseased.

"Jesus therefore went up into a mountain, and there He sat with His disciples.

"Now the Pasch, the festival day of the Jews, was near at hand.

"When Jesus therefore had lifted up his eyes, and seen that a very great multitude cometh to Him, He said to Philip: Whence shall we buy bread, that these may eat?

"And this He said to try him; for He Himself knew what He would do.

"Philip answered Him: Two hundred pennyworth of bread is not sufficient for them, that every one may take a little.

"One of His disciples, Andrew, the brother of Simon Peter, saith to Him:

"There is a boy here that hath five barley loaves, and two fishes; but what are these among so many?

"Then Jesus said: Make the men sit down. Now there was much grass in the place. The men therefore sat down, in number about five thousand.

"And Jesus took the loaves: and when He had given thanks, He distributed to them that were set down. In like manner also of the fishes, as much as they would.

"And when they were filled, He said to his disciples: Gather up the fragments that remain, lest they be lost.

"They gathered up therefore, and filled twelve baskets with the fragments of the five barley loaves, which remained over and above to them that had eaten.

"Now those men, when they had seen what a miracle Jesus had done, said: This is of a truth the Prophet, that is to come into the world." (St. John vi, 1–14.)

THE JOURNEYS OF JESUS

THE DESERT PLACE

The "desert place apart," to which the Saviour invited His Apostles, was about three miles northeast of where the Jordan flows into the Sea of Galilee. This "desert place" is said by some to be the Bethsaida-Julias, so named by the Tetrarch Philip in honor of Julia, the daughter of the Emperor Augustus.

QUESTIONS

1. Where was the desert place to which Jesus took His disciples?

2. What did Philip think it would cost to feed the multitude?

3. How did Christ feed them?

4. What three actions of Jesus on this occasion take place at every Holy Mass?

5. What Sacrament is prefigured in the First Multiplication of Loaves?

XIV

JESUS CROSSES THE LAKE TO BETHSAIDA

Jesus Walks on the Water

The day of the first multiplication of loaves ended and left our Blessed Saviour tired and "alone on the land, alone with His Heavenly Father." He had sent His disciples "before Him over the water to Bethsaida, whilst He dismissed the people. And when He had dismissed them, He went up to the mountain to pray." (St. Mark vi, 45–46.)

"But the boat [of the disciples] in the midst of the sea was tossed with the waves: for the wind was contrary.

"And in the fourth watch of the night, He came to them walking upon the sea.

"And they seeing Him walking upon the sea, were troubled, saying: It is an apparition. And they cried out for fear.

"And immediately Jesus spoke to them, saying: Be of good heart: It is I, fear ye not.

"And Peter making answer, said: Lord, if it be Thou, bid me come to Thee upon the waters.

JESUS WALKING UPON THE SEA

JESUS CROSSES THE LAKE TO BETHSAIDA

"And He said: Come. And Peter going down out of the boat, walked upon the water to come to Jesus.

"But seeing the wind strong, he was afraid: and when he began to sink, he cried out, Lord, save me.

"And immediately Jesus stretching forth His hand took hold of him, and said to him: O thou of little faith, why didst thou doubt?

"And when they were come up into the boat, the wind ceased.

"And they that were in the boat came and adored Him, saying: Indeed Thou art the Son of God." (St. Matthew xiv, 24–33.)

QUESTIONS

1. After the multiplication of loaves, where did Jesus and the Apostles go?

2. On that night what happened on the sea?

3. Can you give a reason why Jesus said to Peter: "O thou of little faith"?

4. Why did the Apostles say to Jesus, "Indeed, Thou art the Son of God"?

XV

JESUS IN THE LAND OF GENESARETH

The Land of Genesareth

The land of Genesareth was on the western shore of the lake of the same name and extended two miles westward from it. It was an extremely fertile plain. Palm, fig, and olive trees, as well as nut trees, grew there in abundance. The grapes and the figs were plentiful for ten months in the year. Its soil welcomed every kind of tree and shrub. Because of this pleasant climate and rich fertility many people lived there.

Jesus Promises the Eucharistic Bread

The crowds that had been fed in the wilderness by the loving Saviour had watched the ship of the Apostles drawing off from the shore and had seen that Jesus had not embarked with them, "but that His disciples were gone away alone." They speedily sought Him, but lost all trace of Him in the darkness of the night. At early dawn they again searched, but failed to find Him. They came to the conclusion that He had gone by land over some less-frequented road, intending to rejoin His Apostles in the land of Genesareth.

"Other ships came in from Tiberias; nigh unto the place where they had eaten the bread, the Lord giving thanks"; in these ships many of the people "took shipping, and came to Capharnaum, seeking for Jesus."

On their arrival they found the Lord on the other side of the sea and "they said to Him: Rabbi, when camest Thou hither?

"Jesus answered them, and said: Amen, amen I say to you, you seek Me, not because you have seen miracles, but because you did eat of the loaves, and were filled.

"Labour not for the meat which perisheth, but for that which endureth unto life everlasting, which the Son of Man will give you. For Him hath God, the Father, sealed.

"They said therefore unto Him: What shall we do, that we may work the works of God?

"Jesus answered, and said to them: This is the work of God, that you believe in Him Whom He hath sent.

"They said therefore to Him: What sign therefore dost Thou show, that we may see, and may believe Thee? What dost Thou work?

"Our fathers did eat manna in the desert, as it is written: *He gave them bread from heaven to eat.*

"Then Jesus said to them: Amen, amen I say to you: Moses gave you not bread from heaven, but My Father giveth you the true bread from heaven.

"For the bread of God is that which cometh down from heaven, and giveth life to the world.

"They said therefore unto Him: Lord, give us always this bread.

"And Jesus said to them: I am the Bread of Life: he that cometh to Me shall not hunger: and he that believeth in Me shall never thirst.

"But I said unto you, that you also have seen Me, and you believe not.

"All that the Father giveth to Me shall come to Me; and him that cometh to Me, I will not cast out.

"Because I am come down from heaven, not to do My own will, but the will of Him that sent Me.

"Now this is the will of the Father who sent Me: that of all that He hath given Me, I should lose nothing; but should raise it up again in the last day,

"And this is the will of My Father that sent Me: that every one who seeth the Son, and believeth in Him, may have life everlasting, and I will raise him up in the last day." (St. John vi, 22–40.)

JESUS IN THE LAND OF GENESARETH

QUESTIONS

1. What is meant by saying "Jesus promised the Eucharistic Bread"?

2. Where was Jesus at the time of this promise?

3. What can you tell of the manna that fell in the desert?

4. Of what was the manna a figure?

THE JEWS MURMUR

"The Jews therefore murmured at Him, because He had said: I am the living Bread which came down from heaven.

"And they said: Is not this Jesus, the son of Joseph, whose father and mother we know? How then saith He, I came down from heaven?

"Jesus therefore answered, and said to them: Murmur not among yourselves.

"No man can come to Me, except the Father, Who hath sent Me, draw him; and I will raise him up in the last day.

"It is written in the Prophets: *And they shall all be taught of God.* Every one that hath heard of the Father, and hath learned, cometh to Me.

"Not that any man hath seen the Father; but He Who is of God, He hath seen the Father.

[189]

"Amen, amen I say unto you: He that believeth in Me, hath everlasting life.

"I am the Bread of Life.

"Your fathers did eat manna in the desert, and are dead.

"This is the Bread which cometh down from heaven; that if any man eat of it, he may not die.

"I am the living Bread which came down from heaven.

"If any man eat of this Bread, he shall live for ever; and the Bread that I will give, is My flesh, for the Life of the world.

"The Jews therefore strove among themselves, saying: How can this Man give us His flesh to eat?

"Then Jesus said to them: Amen, amen I say unto you: Except you eat the flesh of the Son of Man, and drink His blood, you shall not have Life in you.

"He that eateth My flesh, and drinketh My blood, hath everlasting Life: and I will raise him up in the last day.

"For My flesh is meat indeed: and My blood is drink indeed.

"He that eateth My flesh, and drinketh My blood, abideth in Me, and I in him.

"As the Living Father hath sent Me, and I live by the Father; so he that eateth Me, the same also shall live by Me.

JESUS IN THE LAND OF GENESARETH

"This is the Bread that came down from heaven. Not as your fathers did eat manna, and are dead. He that eateth this Bread, shall live for ever.

"These things He said, teaching in the synagogue, in Capharnaum.

"Many therefore of His disciples, hearing it, said: This saying is hard, and who can hear it?

"But Jesus, knowing in Himself, that His disciples murmured at this, said to them: Doth this scandalize you?

"If then you shall see the Son of Man ascend up where He was before?

"It is the spirit that quickeneth: the flesh profiteth nothing. The words that I have spoken to you, are spirit and life." (St. John vi, 41–64.)

QUESTIONS

1. Why did Jesus send His Apostles across the lake immediately after the Miracle of Loaves?

2. What was the next miracle after the First Multiplication of Loaves?

3. Where did Jesus spend the night of that day?

4. Why do you think Jesus worked these two miracles at this time?

5. Which miracle did the Apostles think the greater?

6. Which do you think the greater?

7. Which one concerns us more nearly?

THE JOURNEYS OF JESUS

Jesus Foretells His Betrayal by Judas

"But there are some of you that believe not. For Jesus knew from the beginning, who they were that did not believe, and who he was, that would betray Him.

"And He said: Therefore did I say to you, that no man can come to Me, unless it be given him by My Father.

"After this many of His disciples went back; and walked no more with Him. (St. John vi, 65–67.)

However, the twelve Apostles remained with the Divine Saviour. Turning to them in His grief, He said to the Twelve: "Will you also go away?

"And Simon Peter answered Him: "Lord, to whom shall we go? Thou hast the words of eternal life.

"And we have believed and have known, that Thou art the Christ, the Son of God.

"Jesus answered them: Have not I chosen you Twelve; and one of you is a devil?

"Now He meant Judas Iscariot, the son of Simon: for this same was about to betray Him, whereas he was one of the Twelve." (St. John vi, 68–72.)

This gentle rebuke of the Saviour did not win over Judas. Though he continued in the company of Jesus he had already betrayed Him in his soul.

JESUS IN THE LAND OF GENESARETH

Jesus, finding Judas unmoved by His words of warning, sadly went away from the synagogue.

QUESTIONS

1. After Jesus promised the Holy Eucharist many of His disciples left Him. Give a reason for their doing so.

2. What profession did Peter make at this time when so many went away from Jesus?

3. Do you think that all the Apostles knew whom Jesus meant when He said to them, "One of you is a devil"?

BIBLICAL GLOSSARY

A List of the Most Important Names Used in
"The Journeys of Jesus"

Key. făt, fāte, ärm, sofạ, mĕt, mēte, ênough, hēr, novẹl, ĭt, īce, nŏt, nōte, melọn, fŏŏt, fōōd, ŭp, ūse, ûrn, stirrụp.

Andrew (ăn'drōō) : one of the twelve Apostles and the brother of Peter.

Archelaus (är'kê lā'ụs) : the son of Herod the Great.

Arimathea (ăr'ĭ mạ thē'ạ) : a town in Judea, the home of Joseph who begged the Body of Christ for burial.

Bartholomew (bär thŏl'ô mū) : one of the Apostles, thought to be Nathanael.

Beatitudes (bê ăt'ĭ tūdz), **Mount of:** the mount on which Christ sat when He gave the great sermon on the Beatitudes.

Bethabara (bĕth ăb'ạ rạ) : a place supposed to be on the east side of the Jordan, between the Dead Sea and the Sea of Galilee. It is thought that Jesus was baptized at this ford.

Bethany (bĕth'ạ nĭ) : a village two miles from Jerusalem on the eastern slope of Mount Olivet.

Bethsaida-Julias (bĕth sā'ĭ dạ jool'yạs) : the "desert place apart" to which the Saviour invited His Apostles.

Cana (kā'nạ) : a village in Galilee near Nazareth.

Capharnaum (kạ fär'nả ụm) : a town in Galilee on the north-western shore of the Sea of Galilee.

Cedron (sē'drọn), or **Kedron** (kē'drọn) : the brook on the eastern side of the city of Jerusalem.

[195]

BIBLICAL GLOSSARY

Cephas (sē'fạs) : a name given to Simon Peter by Christ.

Chusa (kū'zạ) : the steward of Herod Antipas. His wife, Joanna, was one of the women who ministered to Christ.

Cleophas (klē'ô făs) : supposed to be the same as Alpheus.

Cubit (kū'bĭt) : a measure of length used among the Jews, the distance from the elbow to the tip of the middle finger, or about eighteen inches.

David (dā'vĭd) : the greatest of all the kings who ruled Israel. He was born 1085 B.C. and ruled for forty years, from 1050 until 1010 B.C.

Decapolis (dĕ kăp'ô lĭs) : a portion of Palestine mainly on the east side of the Jordan; it contained ten cities.

Elias (ê lī'ạs), or **Elijah** (ê lī'jạ) : one of the great prophets of the Old Testament.

Elizabeth (ê lĭz'ạ bĕth) : the wife of Zachary and the mother of St. John the Baptist.

Eucharist (ū'kạ rĭst) : the Sacrament of the Body and Blood of Christ.

Evangelist (ê văn'jĕl ĭst) : a word used to describe those who wrote the Gospels.

Galilee (găl'ĭ lē) : the most northern of the provinces of Palestine at the time of Christ.

Galilee, Sea of: a lake named from the province of Galilee, twelve or fourteen miles long and six or seven miles wide. Called also Sea of Chinnereth, Lake of Genesareth, and Sea of Tiberias.

Genesareth (gĕ nĕs'ạ rĕth), **Lake of:** the Sea of Galilee.

Gentile (jĕn'tīl) : the name given by the Jews to all who did not know the true God.

Gentiles, Court of the: the outer court of the Temple, where the uncircumcised could stand during services.

BIBLICAL GLOSSARY

Gerasa (gĕr'ạ sạ) : the city of Decapolis in which Jesus cured the demoniac.

Gergesa (gûr'gĕ sạ) : a city on the Sea of Galilee.

Gerizim (gĕr'ĭ zĭm) : a mountain in Ephrem near Shechem, from which blessings were pronounced. It was the site of the first Samaritan temple.

Hattin (hăt'tĭn), **Horns of:** peaks on the Mount of Beatitudes, so called because of the small cones on the ridge. They took the name from the village of Hattin near the base of the mountain.

Hebrews (hē'brōōz) : the name given to all the descendants of Jacob. They were called also Israelites and Jews.

Hebron (hē'brụn) : an ancient royal city of Chanaan famous in Biblical history, especially at the time of the patriarchs and of David.

Hermon (hēr'mọn), **Mount:** a high peak in the southern part of the mountain range of Anti-Libanus, north of the Sea of Galilee.

Herod Antipas (hĕr'ụd ăn'tĭ pạs) : the son of Herod the Great. After his father's death he ruled the tetrarchy of Galilee and Perea.

Herod the Great: the second son of Antipater and the tyrant who massacred the Innocents. He became king of Judea in 40 B.C.

Herodias (hĕ rō'dĭ ăs) : the unlawful wife of Herod.

Hinnom (hĭn'ọm) : a valley to the south and west of Jerusalem. The term *Gehenna* (Ge Hinnom), hell, comes from the name of this valley.

Holy of holies: the most sacred place in the Temple, where the Ark of the Lord was placed.

Holy Place: a place outside the Holy of holies and separated from it by the veil of the Temple.

Holy Spirit: the Third Person of the Most Holy Trinity.

BIBLICAL GLOSSARY

Idumea (Ĭd ū mē′a̦) : a region in Judea.

Isaias (ī zā′ya̦s) : one of the great prophets.

Israel (Ĭz′rȧ ĕl) : the surname of Jacob. It is also used for the whole race of the Hebrews.

Jacob (jā′ku̦b), **Well of:** a well in the territory purchased by Jacob.

Jairus (jā′ĭ ru̦s) : a ruler in the Jewish synagogue; his child was healed by Christ.

James (jāmz) : one of the three favorite Apostles, the brother of John and the son of Zebedee.

James the Lesser: one of the Apostles, the son of Alpheus and Mary.

Jericho (jĕr′ĭ kō) : an ancient city in the valley of the Jordan, about six miles north of the Dead Sea.

Jerusalem (jĕ roō′sa̦ lĕm) : the capital of Palestine, thirty-two miles from the Mediterranean and eighteen miles from the river Jordan.

John: the beloved disciple, son of Zebedee, and brother of James.

John the Baptist: the son of Zachary and Elizabeth, and the herald of Christ.

Jona (jō′na̦) : the father of St. Peter, who was called Simon Bar-Jona.

Jordan (jôr′da̦n) : the only river in Palestine, rising in Mount Hermon and emptying into the Dead Sea.

Joseph (jō′zĕf) : the espoused husband of the Virgin Mary and foster-father of Christ; a carpenter of Nazareth.

Joseph of Arimathea: a wealthy man, a member of the Sanhedrin, who became a disciple of Christ.

Josue (jŏs′ū ē) : the son of Nun of the Tribe of Ephraim, who became the successor of Moses.

Judas, or **Thaddeus** (thăd′ĕ u̦s) : one of the Apostles, a brother of James; also called Jude.

BIBLICAL GLOSSARY

Judas Iscariot (jōō′dạs ĭs kăr′ĭ ọt) : one of the twelve Apostles, the one who betrayed Christ.

Judea (jōō dē′ạ) : a province of Palestine.

Kedron. *See* Cedron.

Levi (lē′vī) : one of the Apostles, also called Matthew.

Levites (lē′vīts) : the descendants of Levi, who served the priests in the Temple. The priests were Levites, but they were always descendants of Aaron also.

Machærus (mă kē′rŭs) : the fortress in which John the Baptist was imprisoned.

Manna (măn′ạ) : the food supplied by God to the Jews in the wilderness.

Mark (märk) : one of the Evangelists, a disciple of St. Peter.

Mary Magdalen (măg′dạ lĕn) : a sinful woman who was converted by Christ.

Matthew (măth′ū) : one of the twelve Apostles, the writer of the first Gospel.

Mediterranean (mĕd ĭ tēr ā′nĕ ạn) : the Great Sea, as it is called in Scripture, enclosed by Europe, Asia, and Africa.

Messias (mẹ sī′ạs) : the term applied to Christ as the One sent by God for man's redemption.

Miracle (mĭr′ạ k'l) : a supernatural event brought about in nature by the power of God.

Moses (mō′zĕz) : the great law-giver of the Jews, son of Amram and Jochabed of the Tribe of Levi.

Naim (nā′ĭm) : a town in Galilee.

Nathanael (nạ thăn′ả ĕl) : one of Christ's disciples. He came from Cana in Galilee and is thought to be Bartholomew.

Nazareth (năz′ạ rĕth) : a town in Galilee about seventy miles from Jerusalem.

BIBLICAL GLOSSARY

Nicodemus (nĭk ô dē′mụs) : a ruler of the Jews, a Pharisee, who sought Christ and became His follower.

Palestine (păl′ĕs tīn) : the Holy Land, bounded on the north by Syria, on the east by the river Euphrates and the Great Desert, on the south by Negeb, and on the west by the Mediterranean.

Parable (păr′ạ b′l) : a story told to teach a truth.

Pasch (păsk) : the feast of the Passover among the Jews — a term later applied to Easter.

Passover (păs′ō vēr) : the principal feast of the Jews, reminding them of the sparing of the families of the Israelites when the destroying angel killed the first-born of Egypt.

Pennyworth (pĕn′ĭ wûrth) : as much as could be bought with a penny, a Roman silver coin worth about sixteen cents of our money. In the time of Jesus, a penny was a day's wages.

Perea (pĕ rē′ạ) : a territory to the east of the Jordan between the Sea of Galilee and the Dead Sea.

Pharisees (făr′ĭ sēz) : a religious sect among the Jews.

Philip (fĭl′ĭp) : an Apostle from Bethsaida.

Quarantaine (kwŏr ăn tān′) : the mountain where it is said that Christ permitted the great temptation.

Rabbi (răb′ī) : a title of respect given by the Jews to the doctors of the law.

Sadducees (săd′ů sēz) : a religious sect among the Jews.

Salome (sạ lō′mĕ) : the daughter of Herodias, who as a reward for her dancing before Herod was granted the head of John the Baptist.

Samaria (sạ mā′rĭ ạ) : the central province of Palestine, south of Galilee and north of Judea.

[200]

BIBLICAL GLOSSARY

Samaritan (sạ măr'ĭ tạn) : a native of Samaria.

Sanhedrin (săn'hĕ drĭn) : the great council of the Jews.

Scribes (skrībz) : writers among the Jews, copyists and explainers of the Law.

Scythopolis (sī thŏp'ŏ lĭs) : the principal city of the region known as Decapolis.

Shechem (shē'kĕm) : a town in the valley between Mounts Hebal and Gerizim, called also Sichem.

Shiloah (shĭ lō'ạ) : a brook south of Jerusalem.

Sichar (sī'kär) : a Samaritan city where Jesus talked with the woman of Samaria at Jacob's Well.

Simon Peter (sī'mọn pē'tēr) : the chief of the Apostles, whose name was Simon, afterwards changed to Peter.

Simon Zelotes (zĕ lō'tēz) : one of the twelve Apostles. He is called Zelotes (or the Zealot) to distinguish him from St. Peter, whose original name was Simon.

Synagogue (sĭn'ạ gŏg) : the meeting place of the Jews.

Temple (tĕm'p'l) : the chief place of worship among the Jews, erected upon Mount Moriah, in Jerusalem.

Thaddeus. *See* Judas.

Thomas (tŏm'ạs) : one of the twelve Apostles, called also Didymus.

Tiberius (tī bē'rĭ ụs) : a Roman emperor, the stepson and successor of Augustus. He lived from 42 B.C. to A.D. 37.

Zachary (zăk'ạ rĭ) : the husband of Elizabeth and the father of John the Baptist.

Zebedee (zĕb'ĕ dē) : the father of the Apostles James the Greater and John.

Zion (zī'ọn), **Mount of :** the southwestern hill of Jerusalem.

9781640511323